# CONCILIUM

## THEOLOGY IN THE AGE OF RENEWAL

# CONCILIUM

# CONCILIUM/VOL. 44

# ECUMENICAL THEOLOGY

# THE FUTURE
# OF
# ECUMENISM

edited by HANS KÜNG

# VOLUME 44

# *CONCILIUM*
*theology in the age of renewal*

PAULIST PRESS
NEW YORK, N.Y./PARAMUS, N.J.

PAULIST PRESS
EXECUTIVE OFFICES: 304 W. 58th Street, New York, N.Y. and 404
    Sette Drive, Paramus, N.J.
*Publisher:* John A. Carr, C.S.P.


EDITORIAL OFFICES: 304 W. 58th Street, New York, N.Y.
*Executive Editor:* Kevin A. Lynch, C.S.P.
*Managing Editor:* Urban P. Intondi


Printed and bound in the United States of America by
Wickersham Printing Co., Lancaster, Pa.

# CONTENTS

## PART II

## BIBLIOGRAPHICAL SURVEY

## PART III

### DOCUMENTATION CONCILIUM
Office of the Executive Secretary
*Nijmegen, Netherlands*

# PREFACE

Hans Küng/*Tübingen, West Germany*

**M**any Christians experience a certain impatience today, and they are not only found among the young or in the Catholic Church. This is a healthy sign, for apart from all unholy impatience, there is also, as the prophets, St. Paul and Jesus himself have shown, a holy impatience which sees God's will in that something must be done *now,* and must really be *done.* All too often we are content with merely picking up the plow (or discussing whether we should pick it up). We still will not let the dead bury the dead in theology.

In ecumenism we talk too much and do too little. One can understand the growing impatience, particularly among the younger generation in Europe and North America, who want to get down to concrete action and practical arrangements. Theological discussion is no doubt necessary, both before and after; otherwise we would become involved in an unenlightened, wild and contradictory ecumenical activism which would do Christian unity more harm than good in the long run. But this unenlightened ecumenical activism is precisely provoked by a theological discussion that goes around in circles, drags one foot after another in a slow and dull movement, remains abstract and seems to be barely affected by the concrete needs and worries of the people and the Churches. If theology really wants to discharge its

1

function in the service of these people and these Churches, it must have a firm determination to follow up its theoretical conclusions with theologically responsible practical solutions which actively foster ecumenical understanding.

The present volume of *Concilium* seeks to take a few essential steps in this direction. In a previous volume we have already dealt with mixed marriages. The solution of this problem which recognizes the validity of all mixed marriages and leaves the decision about the education of the children and their baptism to the informed conscience of the parents has been treated exhaustively; rather than further theoretical development, it needs only a speedy and practical decision. But apart from this question of mixed marriages, there are many other points which badly need to be discussed and then to be brought to a practical conclusion. The future must be investigated in a practical sense, and without the courage to experiment we shall not make any significant progress. Furthermore, since this courage must be enlightened and the experimenting must be done responsibly, theology must turn its attention to actual practice. In this way we shall realize that the ecumenical future is not a utopia, but a real possibility which only needs to be faced with determination.

In order that the reader should not lose sight of the forest for the trees, let us here enumerate the requirements which the Catholic Church together with the other Christian Churches can and must courageously put into practice:

1. Unconditional and mutual recognition of each other's baptism.

2. Regular exchange of preachers, catechists and professors of theology so that we can become acquainted with what we have in common and on what we disagree.

3. More frequent (and not only exceptional) common services of the Word, already allowed, and an investigation of the conditions required for a common eucharist.

4. More freedom with regard to participation in services in other Christian Churches (particularly in the case of mixed marriages).

5. As far as possible, the common use of churches and the setting up of common churches and presbyteries.

6. The regulation of the question of mixed marriages by the recognition of the validity of all mixed marriages and the leaving of the decision about education and baptism to the conscience of the partners (an ecumenical marriage rite).

7. The fostering of common biblical study in the communities and at the academic level (common translations and commentaries).

8. Increased cooperation and integration in the denominational theological faculties (building up common libraries for seminaries, common educational organization, mutual recognition of lectures and projects).

9. Investigation of possibilities for establishing a common theological and ecumenical center for basic studies.

10. Ecumenical cooperation in public life (common attitudes to certain issues, common initiatives and action).

Finally, a brief observation about the word which seems still to irritate many a Catholic theologian: courage. How can the pope, the bishop and the theologian show courage in ecumenical matters? Many of those who were invited to contribute to this volume pointed out that "courage" would imply "prudence", "caution", "moderation" and so on. This was probably not due to the fact that, in the French translation of the circular sent out at that time, "mut" was translated by "audace" instead of simply "courage". It is rather that in Catholic theology there is always a certain nervousness when "courage" is mentioned. Should it not have been obvious to theologians that this courage must be prudent, cautious and moderate, or, as I put it, "enlightened"? In any case, for too long a time have "moderation" (*temperantia*) and "cautiousness" (*prudentia*) been singled out among the cardinal virtues for the situation in the Church and in theology, while "courage" (*fortitudo*) was barely mentioned, as if one could be truly "prudent" without being "courageous". A "balanced" man seemed to represent the highest ideal of a Christian and a theologian, even when this was linked with an utterly boring, utterly sterile theology, totally alien to the Gospel. When the balance has been destroyed, one can hardly afford too much moderation. The prophets, St. Paul and Jesus himself were not exactly nicely balanced bourgeois people. What we need today in theology and in the Church is *enlightened courage:* courage to think, courage to act and courage to experiment in ecumenical matters.

This is not a call to major or minor revolutions in theology, which can only encourage ecclesiastical and political reactionism. But it *does* mean a call to a realistic, effective, prudent and courageous reform and renewal. The guiding principle must be the original message of Jesus Christ himself. The scope stretches as far as the world. The aim is man, for whom we are theologians and pastors. The source of our strength, the hope of our fulfillment, the Alpha and Omega of all we do, of our theology and our practice, of our progress and our attempts, of true stability when confronted with ecclesiastical pressure and theological dangers, is God, the Lord of the world and the Lord of the Church, and he alone.

# PART I
## ARTICLES

Jean-Jacques von Allmen/*Neuchâtel, Switzerland*

# The Conditions for an Acceptable Intercommunion

## I
### THE GROWING DESIRE FOR INTERCOMMUNION

People on both sides of the denominational barriers are currently taking part in eucharistic celebrations held in churches of which they are not members. And as time goes on, more and more of us are wondering what prevents us from sharing communion on such occasions. Increasingly we are forced to admit that it is due to a purely disciplinary reason. We do not share communion on such occasions because we do not have the authorization, not because we have any theological or spiritual qualms about doing so.

Even if the format of the ritual is a bit strange to us, what we see taking place seems to correspond closely enough to what we know about the eucharistic mystery in our own Church. As a result, we wonder why these two Churches do not mutually recognize their respective eucharists as the same Christian eucharist and accept communicants from both Churches without taking note of the divisions between them. Instead of sneaking off to a eucharistic celebration in a church to which we do not belong, instead of feeling inwardly resentful of a prohibition which we no longer understand, wouldn't it be better to permit a reciprocal eucharistic hospitality?

7

It should not surprise anyone that this question is being asked by an ever increasing number of Christians. There has been a widespread renovation in eucharistic doctrine, liturgy and practice. Historical circumstances have changed, showing us that the divisions among Christians bear the stamp of the time in which they arose to a large extent, and that our era is a different one. Thus the Churches must ask themselves whether eucharistic discipline should not be reformed as well. And there are even more serious questions to be answered. Has the time not come to say and to prove, with acts of prophetic impudence if necessary, that the things which divide the Churches are no longer weighty enough to justify the breakoff of communion in our present circumstances? Is it not time to show that the maintenance of Christian denominations, in opposition or juxtaposition to one another, is less and less defensible?

Two further reasons suggest why we cannot avoid posing the question of intercommunion. First of all, the overwhelming majority of the faithful go to communion for reasons that would not prevent them from doing so together. They go to communion to obey the will of Christ, to be nourished by his life, to obtain pardon, to get beyond the things which create opposition between human beings, to profess that they love Christ and those for whom he died, and to pledge that they will bear witness to him in their daily life. They do not go to communion primarily because of what the catechism says about the reality of Christ's presence at the Last Supper, or about the connection between the cross and its sacramental commemoration. Nor do they go to communion primarily to signify that they recognize, in those who invite them to the Lord's supper, the right to do this in Christ's name.

The second reason is the strongest of all. At present, Church authorities are committing the faithful to efforts at ecumenical dialogue. They cannot help but see that these efforts are really so many prayers, and that sharing in the eucharist would be the answer to them. They are inviting the members of separated

Churches to pardon each other, to hear the Word of God in joint assemblies, to discuss their points of agreement and disagreement, to collaborate in common actions of service or the apostolate, and to pray together. They would be blind to the workings of the Holy Spirit if they did not expect all this to lead to an ever stronger and clearer appeal for the realization of unity and for joint sharing of the eucharistic bread and wine by those who look forward to this unity. To develop a taste for unity among separated Christians is more than a passing fancy. It involves a risk: the risk of seeing unity become a reality.

But does this mean that intercommunion is acceptable? In principle, no. Theologically speaking, victory over our divisions is not achieved by intercommunion (which disregards a division *that still exists*), but by communion (which ratifies and confirms our successful overcoming of divisiveness). But the concrete decisions connected with this process involve so many non-theological factors that a theologically pure solution seems highly improbable. Therefore, we must regard intercommunion as an admissible anomaly.

If we wanted to reject any and all *intercommunion,* we would have to be able to promise something else to those who longed for it: namely, that they would be able to enjoy *communion* in the near future. We would have to be able to put some date on that promise, and to have reasonable hopes of keeping it. But if we cannot set a time limit on the patience required, we have no right to expect that people will wait patiently for full communion.

Now the fact is that Church authorities still see many obstacles on the road to unity. They are not yet in a position to set a date for its achievement. They do not want to break off the quest for unity (how could they?), nor do they feel free to barge through the obstacles that remain without a second thought. This being the case, the conditions for an acceptable intercommunion are something that we cannot avoid.

## II
### SPECIFYING THE CONDITIONS

1. Intercommunion is acceptable if it is not confused with the reattainment of unity in the Church but is recognized as simply a step toward this end. We must acknowledge that intercommunion does not resolve the problem at its roots. Rather, it helps us to be patient by giving us a foretaste of the unity we seek in history, even as the eucharist itself gives us a foretaste of the heavenly kingdom.

To be sure, we cannot meet each other at the eucharist and then separate from each other once again with impunity. An event like the eucharist normally presupposes the mutual exchange of the kiss of peace. But many varied factors condition the divisions between us, and some of them are not directly concerned with the points at issue or subject to the immediate disposition of the Churches and their authorities. We can readily admit, therefore, that the will of Christ, the faith we share, the love which summons Christ's followers together, and the desire to bear common witness to the world may weigh more heavily on the scale than the things which divide us. For the latter are tinged with a trace of bitterness that derives from a past historical and cultural situation rather than from our own circumstances today.

For intercommunion to be acceptable, then, we must solemnly acknowledge that it is simply a means toward our goal—not the goal itself. While the faithful rejoice over the possibility of sharing "the fountainhead and high point of the whole Christian life" (*Constitution on the Church,* n. 11), they must not feel that the goal has been reached simply because they are at the summit together. Nor should intercommunion allow clergy and laity to rest content with an occasional unity and to neglect the other aspects of ecclesial structure and life that are necessarily bound up with the eucharistic celebration. They must not entertain the erroneous notion that these other aspects do not affect the fidelity of the Church. Intercommunion should not perpetuate Christian disunity; rather, it should make it even more intolerable.

2. Intercommunion is acceptable if it is authorized and supervised. Intercommunion, like full communion, is not something we can exproprate for ourselves; it is a mystery into which we are admitted. Like the widow who importuned the wicked judge for justice, we must perseveringly plead for it.

If we engage in intercommunion on the sly, our satisfaction will be rather egotistical and questionable. In such a case, intercommunion will do very little to hasten the restoration of unity. That is why intercommunion as such is not acceptable. It is only acceptable when it is agreed upon by two Churches, consciously separated from one another, that are concretely structured in their credal profession and their locale.[1]

3. Intercommunion is acceptable when it involves some minimal formulation of the points at issue between the two Churches. It cannot be authorized if it is going to create a grave spiritual danger for those who are supposed to benefit from it.

To make this point clear, let me review briefly the eucharistic debate between the Roman Catholic Church and the Calvinist Church. The Heidelberg Catechism of 1563, the classic catechism of Calvinism, sets up the following opposition between "the Lord's supper" and "the Papist Mass":

> The Lord's supper teaches us that we have the full remission of all our sins through the unique sacrifice of Jesus Christ, which he offered once for all on the cross; and that,

[1] The local assembly is the "preeminent manifestation" of the Church of God, as the conciliar *Constitution on the Sacred Liturgy* so rightly observes (n. 41). That is why I have limited my discussion here to intercommunion on the local level, without treating all the nuances. I am thinking specifically of intercommunion between the Calvinist Church and the Roman Catholic Church, as they exist in Switzerland. I realize that the problem of intercommunion exists on many other levels, but I have chosen not to consider them here.

through the Holy Spirit, we have been incorporated into Christ, who now sits bodily at the right hand of the Father in heaven and wants our adoration.

The Mass, on the other hand, teaches people that the living and the dead do not have the remission of sins through the passion of Jesus Christ, unless Christ is sacrificed every day for them by the priest celebrant. And it teaches that Christ is present bodily under the appearances of bread and wine, and therefore is to be adored under those forms. Thus the Mass, in essence, is nothing else but the denial of Christ's unique passion and sacrifice, and an abominable idolatry. (Question 80)

Now someone may say that this catechism, which once was a pedagogical manual and a credal profession of faith, has fallen into disuse in many Calvinist churches. But, to my knowledge, we have never publicly stated that its description of the Mass is unfair or incorrect. And if the "papist" celebration of the eucharist is truly as the catechism describes it, we could not possibly ask Calvinist ecclesiastical authorities to allow Calvinists to attend communion in a Roman Catholic church.

What we must do is find out if Roman Catholics recognize their eucharist in our description of it, thus giving them an opportunity to change our opinion and to show us the Calvinists will not go astray by attending communion in Roman Catholic churches.

On the Catholic side, Vatican Council II's *Decree on Ecumenism* has this reservation about Protestant Churches (which would include our Calvinist Church): "We believe that they have not retained the complete and genuine substance of the mystery of the eucharist, especially because of their lack of the sacrament of orders" (n. 22).

In short, while the Decree has many positive things to say about our eucharist—we are far from the brutal crudities of the 16th century—it does not allow our eucharist the right to be regarded wholly as the repast instituted by Christ. Why? Because it allegedly lacks one of the elements which would enable us to recognize it as the meal willed by Christ, and to derive from it the effects intended by him: it is not presided over by a man who can legitimately claim to be the representative of Christ himself. Thus it is not certain that this service is the Lord's supper; there is, at the very least, some doubt about it.

Now if this is how things stand, we cannot expect Roman Catholic authorities to allow their members to approach the communion table in a Calvinist church. Catholics, therefore, must find out if we recognize our ministers of Christ in their description of them, thus giving us a chance to change their opinion and to show them that Roman Catholics will not go astray by attending communion in Calvinist churches.

4. Intercommunion is acceptable when it enjoys authorization from both sides. If reciprocity is lacking, the Church which grants authorization would be in a ticklish situation. The agreeing Church must admit that the other Church is more of a Church than itself, since it accepts the refusing Church's verdict on its own lack of ecclesiality. Or else, to establish its own ecclesiality and to recognize that of other Churches, the agreeing Church must have recourse to different criteria than those which it failed to pass.

In such a situation, intercommunion would be rather relative, and those who took part would come dangerously close to betraying their own denominational beliefs.

5. Intercommunion is acceptable when it is one of the measures adopted by two Churches to further and accelerate their already initiated negotiations for reunion. This point has been well made by T. F. Torrance.[2]

The Lord's supper is the sacrament which not only "manifests" but also "brings about" the unity of the Church.[3] Moreover, negotiations on reunion presuppose some basic reciprocal recognition of ecclesiality. For these reasons, it seems quite legitimate to prepare and facilitate the hoped-for reunion by au-

[2] Cf. "La mission de l'Eglise," in *Verbum Caro* 77 (1966), p. 16.
[3] *Decree on Ecumenism*, n. 2.

thorizing intercommunion and intercelebration for the members (and the ministers) of both Churches. Such authorization would also prevent Church authorities from giving more weight to reasons for breaking off negotiations than to those for continuing them—and there is no small merit in this consideration. The understanding would be that the authorization for intercommunion would be withdrawn if the negotiations for reunion fell through.

6. Dare I mention this point? Intercommunion is acceptable if it enables us to avoid new schisms. We cannot overlook the fact that we live in an atmosphere where there is much tension between the *de facto* Churches and the Church we envision. More and more the existing Churches, with their limited and sectarian beliefs, seem to belong to a past beyond which we must now move. There is a growing temptation to break with all these Churches and to join the "Church of the future" that is being envisioned by members of all Churches.

We are not going to overcome the temptation by strangling the hope. The threat of annihilation will give this hope greater justification for striking out on its own. It will then see itself as the only true path for Christian obedience. It will see denominational rigidity, rather than intercommunion, as the real temptation, and it will condemn as illusory any attempt to effect overall Christian renewal by restricting reform to the confines of one's own denomination.

This being the case, why not make room for something resembling a religious order, approved and regulated by the two Churches involved? The members of this order, dedicated to unity and Church reform, would receive authorization for intercommunion (and intercelebration, if they are ministers).

7. Intercommunion is acceptable if the participants do not mistake or deprecate the eucharistic reforms—doctrinal, liturgical and practical—in their own Church. We have much reason to hope for improvement in the eucharistic celebration of every Church.

We Calvinists, for example, cannot gloss over the unjustifiable and now traditional divorce between the Lord's day and the Lord's supper in our Church by suggesting that we shall only be able to receive communion every Sunday in the united Church of a future day. Roman Catholics, I feel, cannot appeal to this same hope in order to gloss over the cruel hoax that is often practiced on the laity. Cheated of their baptismal rights, they are often deprived of the chalice which is an integral part of the repast instituted by Christ.

A unified Church lies ahead of us and summons us toward it. It will be that much freer and more faithful if it springs from the concerted efforts of Churches which, despite their continuing though transient separation, have made fidelity to Christ their highest ambition and their greatest joy.

Herman Fiolet/*De Bilt, Netherlands*

# Intercommunion: A Catholic Reply

The question about the possibilities of and conditions for intercommunion between Roman Catholics and the Orthodox and Reformed Churches cannot be solved in a uniform theoretical way by a dogmatic comparison of the eucharistic beliefs of these Churches. For centuries the Churches have been checking up on each other's belief and rejecting each other.

This approach excluded any possibility of meeting each other at the one table of the Lord because the eucharist was seen as the sign of *existing* unity. Only an identical confession could give access to the one communion table. In the efforts to overcome this traditional barrier of confession, there is a tendency current at the moment to put intercommunion not at the end of a long road toward unity but at the beginning of that road, a tendency to foster the ecumenical encounter between the Churches by using the eucharist as a means *toward* unity.

This option between the eucharist as the end *or* the beginning is unacceptable. If the Church's unity is assessed by the dogmatic denominator of a confession, and the common meal must remain divided until the divided Christians confess their conviction about the eucharistic event in exactly the same way, then the eucharist simply becomes an ecumenical *fata morgana*. In that case one denies the fact that both Churches and individual Christians today have already discovered their Christ-given unity and are growing toward each other in this living faith. This unity in Christ is really lived today—in however hesitant and broken a manner—and so in one way or another there must be a possibility to celebrate communion together as Christ's saving aid *toward* a growing unity of his Church. On the other hand, if this eucharistic communion in its coexistence with a "played down" division is forced, the danger of ecumenical magic is not entirely imaginary. One expects a sacrament to express ultimately the mission of the Churches and of Christians at large, for an intercommunion which is not the sign of a true unity already experienced between various denominations dulls the awareness of the fact that unity can only be attained by a genuine conversion of both the believing community and the believing individuals.

## A Sign of Existing Unity and of the Road toward Unity

The changes which have taken place in the ecclesial awareness of Roman Catholics as a result of Vatican Council II demand that we overcome this dilemma: intercommunion must signify *both* existing unity and the means toward unity. In the *Constitution on the Church* and the *Decree on Ecumenism,* Roman Catholicism took a long look at the ecclesial values contained in other ecclesial communities. Because of this the Roman Catholic Church can no longer see herself as exclusively—i.e., excluding the other Churches—the Church of Jesus Christ. For, in spite of all the elements that keep the Churches divided, it is the Spirit who dwells in the believer and fills and governs the whole Church. "This Spirit brings about that marvelous communion of the faithful and joins them together so intimately in Christ that he is the principle of the Church's unity" (n. 2). The divisions in the Church of Jesus Christ cannot penetrate into the foundation because the one Spirit, the principle of ecclesial unity, is present and active in all Christian ecclesial communities.

The Council recognizes that Church-building values are

operative in these communities: "The written Word of God, the life of grace, faith, hope and charity, along with other interior gifts of the Holy Spirit and visible elements—all of these, which come from Christ and lead back to him, belong by right to the one Church of Christ" (n. 3). The Council recognizes not only the bond of faith between the individual believer and Christ but also the genuine saving instrumentality of the communities as such when it declares that "the sacred actions" of preaching the Word and administering the sacraments "truly engender the life of grace" (n. 3). The Roman Catholic Church will therefore respect these other ecclesial communities because "the Spirit has not refrained from using them as means of salvation" (n. 3). Although Vatican Council II did not reach the point of frankly recognizing the other communities as "the Church of Jesus Christ", it nevertheless made the whole Roman Catholic Church and particularly many "local" Churches (dioceses) particularly sensitive to the ecclesial values of these communities.

Precisely where these local Churches are privileged to live with the Churches of the Reformation in the same country, they have made discoveries in the field of ecumenism which reach beyond Vatican Council II. In the light of these discoveries, the Roman Catholic Church in Holland has in fact recognized the other ecclesial communities as "the Church of Jesus Christ" by inviting them to its pastoral council, not merely as observers but "as participants who could take part in the pastoral council in ways that agreed with their own religious conviction"; on the other hand, the Catholic Church there has been accepted as a member of the Dutch Council of Churches on equal footing with the others. This practical recognition of each other's ecclesial nature has had the result that the Catholic Church in Holland has been able to achieve official mutual recognition of each other's baptism. The ecumenical evaluation of this gesture is bound to lead in the long run to far-reaching ecclesial and pastoral consequences for the life of the respective Churches. For this official mutual recognition of each other's baptism means that these Churches accept each other's baptismal confession and that these Churches can no longer avoid the issue of intercommunion, since baptism constitutes, by the power of the Lord himself, the condition of access to his eucharistic meal.

## The Responsibility of the Local Church

Vatican Council II's view of the Church as the People of God on the way as a pilgrim people, casts an entirely new light on the question about the possibilities of and conditions for intercommunion. The stance of the Roman Catholic Church is no longer that she regards other Christians as individuals who have separated themselves and must now return unconditionally before they can be admitted to the eucharist. She sees the other ecclesial communities as having a saving instrumentality in their own right and as Churches of Jesus Christ. She can no longer maintain the position of traditional apologetics that in the 11th and 16th centuries vast communities of believers separated themselves from the Roman Church but that this Church has remained nevertheless the one true Church of Jesus Christ. One cannot scripturally maintain that after the separation one specific Church remained exclusively faithful to Christ while all the other Churches ceased to be the instrument of the Lord's salvation. All Churches suffered through this separation. As long as the Christ-given unity is lived in a divided experience, all communities are impaired in their full experience of being the Church of Christ. But the unity in Christ remains a fact even in the midst of divisions, and to the extent that this given unity is still felt as overriding the boundaries of division, intercommunion remains a task that the Churches have to face.

Insofar as this unity is already experienced *de facto* among the various communities, it is not only the *condition* of intercommunion but it also determines the *manner* in which this intercommunion can be celebrated. This situation cannot be judged centrally and uniformly for all countries by Rome. It varies according to country and Church. It must be left to the individual Churches of the Roman Catholic Church to decide whether the relations with the other Churches are of such a nature that intercommunion is possible in one way or another. But this decision must not be taken by the local Church with total disregard for the other local Churches, since, on the basis of their unity, all local Churches are bound to be in constant dialogue with each other, and in regard to this dialogue Rome is the legitimizing center. Nevertheless, the actual decision and responsibilty can only lie with the local Church concerned.

Vatican Council II recognized the responsibility of the local Churches on this point: "In view of the principles recalled above, Eastern Christians who are separated in good faith from the Catholic Church, if they ask of their own accord and have the right dispositions, may be granted the sacraments of penance, the eucharist, and the anointing of the sick. Furthermore, Catholics may ask for these same sacraments from those non-Catholic ministers whose Churches possess valid sacraments, as often as necessity or a genuine spiritual benefit recommends such a course of action, and when access to a Catholic priest is physically or morally impossible" (*Decree on Catholic Churches of the Eastern Rite*, n. 27). This cannot be the unilateral decision of a local Roman Catholic Church. It requires of necessity mutual consultation between the Churches. "Insofar as the reception or administration of the sacraments of penance, the eucharist and the anointing of the sick is concerned, it is most desirable that the local Catholic authority or the episcopal synod or conference will not give its consent to such a participation unless at least the competent local authorities of the Eastern Churches have been consulted and favor such a decision" (*Directorium Oecumenicum*, no. 42).

This admission to the Catholic eucharist is also offered to the Churches of the Reformation, although not without hesitation and still unilaterally: "Since the sacraments are both signs of unity and sources of grace, the Church can, for good reasons, allow a separated brother to receive these sacraments. This admission to the sacraments can be granted in danger of death or in dire necessity (during persecution in prison), if the separated brother or minister asks the Catholic priest of his own accord for these sacraments on condition that he professes a faith in these sacraments which accords with the belief of the Church and has the right disposition. In other emergency cases the bishop or the episcopal conference must decide" (*Directorium Oecumenicum,* n. 55).

On the basis of this responsibility given to them, the bishops of Holland have declared with regard to a mixed marriage: "When the marriage ceremony takes place during the celebration of the eucharist and the non-Catholic partner asks to be admitted to communion, we are prepared to allow this in accordance with n. 8 of the *Decree on Ecumenism* of Vatican Council II, of November 21, 1964, and n. 55 of the *Directorium Oecumenicum* for the execution of the decrees of Vatican Council II on ecumenical matters, of May 14, 1967, if the partner is baptized, can accept the belief of the Catholic Church as it is expressed in the celebration of the eucharist, and is admitted to communion in his own Church" (letter of the Dutch hierarchy to the clergy on mixed marriage, *Katholiek Archief* 23 [1968], pp. 376-77).

## Two-Way Traffic

"A Catholic, however, in the same circumstances can only ask a validly ordained priest for these sacraments" (*Directorium Oecumenicum,* n. 55). This ecumenical one-way traffic in the Roman Catholic Church with regard to the Reformed Churches originates in the rejection by the Protestants of transubstantiation and the sacrificial character of the eucharist. The question is, however, whether this confessional barrier still corresponds to the present practice of faith. The realization that God's revelation in Christ is a saving event stretches well beyond what the Churches confess.

In the eucharist the whole attention of faith is concentrated on the significance of salvation for us in the fact that Christ is still man and comes to us in this meal as the grace-giving glorified Lord. The table at which the Lord sat down with his apostles is pushed forward into countries and centuries through his power. We, too, are invited to sit down at it. And so we are involved in the saving event that seized the apostles that evening through the Lord. By offering them his body for food and his blood for drink under the signs of bread and wine, he involved them in the solitary sacrificial deed of his whole life of obedience and made them partakers in the event of our salvation, his resurrection on Easter morning. "As I, who am sent by the living Father, myself draw life from the Father, so whoever eats me will draw life from me" (Jn. 6, 57). The "happening" of his suffering, death and resurrection becomes reality in our life. We are personally taken up into the historical deeds of his human life, and these deeds concern us all. "And on that day you will explain to your son, 'This is because of what Yahweh did for *me* and *I* came out of Egypt' " (Ex. 13, 8).

This presence of the Lord in the eucharistic supper as the application of the whole of salvation in Christ to us personally can be approached by the believer from various angles. No Christian can embrace the mystery of this "happening" of salvation in its totality. While still on our way toward the Lord, we cannot yet enjoy his presence in its fullness. This tension between the totality of the offer of salvation and a faith still groping in darkness necessarily implies the danger of a one-sided approach to the experience of our eucharistic faith.

This one-sidedness is legitimate as long as it remains *inclusive* —i.e., as long as it does not exclude or reject anything deliberately. According to the changes in his own situation, the individual Christian will fasten upon a particular aspect of this rich event which will dominate his actual experience. This also holds for the various believing communities whose experience of the eucharistic supper will be determined by their indigenous temperament and their contemporary image of society. The perspectives and horizons can therefore shift, become larger or concentrate on specific aspects according to the age and according to the people.

This necessary and legitimate one-sidedness will, however, create divisions in the Church as soon as the eucharist is treated with exclusiveness, at least in appearance. We shall have a schism on our doorstep when a uniformity which excludes all other aspects drives out all pluriformity of experience. In her long history the Church of Jesus Christ knows all about the tragedies created by these kinds of exclusive one-sidedness. They have driven individual Christians and whole Christian communities into opposing conflicts of conscience, and in this misery they have made "the Father's home with many mansions" uninhabitable for each other.

Many Christians query today whether the one-sided attention given to the "how" of Christ's presence in this sacrament (transubstantiation: the essential change of bread and wine) is really still relevant for the practice of faith. Together they want to concentrate on the *fact that* the Lord wants to give himself to his own in this eucharistic meal. The Protestant Christians, too, confess that in this meal "they are fed and refreshed with his true body and blood, even with him truly God and man, the one heavenly bread, through the power of the Holy Spirit" (eucharistic prayer from the eucharistic service of the Dutch Reformed Church, *Dienstboek*, p. 88). Together the divided Christians want to achieve a new understanding of this actively saving presence of Christ in the light of the saving message of the risen Lord's appearance to his apostles. This apparition is the living and tangible proof of the saving nature of his life for us: "Because he remains forever, he can never lose his priesthood. It follows then that his power to save is utterly certain, since he is living forever to intercede for all who come to God through him" (Heb. 7, 24). The experience in faith of this fact of his grace-giving presence pushes the question about the manner in which he was present to his apostles after his resurrection wholly into the background. It is a totally unique presence for which we possess no comparable instance and about which we can say nothing meaningfully. A similar fresh approach is taking place with regard to the sacrificial character of the eucharistic meal.

The Protestant Churches have always been fiercely opposed to this view because they are convinced that this view puts man in the center of this celebration and makes the Church the autonomous subject of this sacrificial action. They felt they had to emphasize strongly that the question is not what we can do but what the Lord does. The key point is that it is the Lord's saving action toward us which comes to us as justification, as forgiveness of sins, as communion with him and as expectation of the fulfillment of salvation. In this celebration the full stress falls on the "ephapax", the "once and for all" that Christ has offered this sacrifice for us. To this we cannot add anything, nor is there any need to do so.

Present Protestant thought, however, now demands more attention for the neglected aspect—namely, that this unilateral deed of God confronts man with the demand for a response in terms of his own personal sacrifice. "I beg you, my brothers, by the mercy of God to offer yourselves as a living, holy sacrifice, truly pleasing to God" (Rom. 12, 1).

On the other hand, Catholics have come to see that their liturgy puts a too one-sided stress on the sacrificial character of the eucharistic mystery and that it overemphasizes the offering of the Church, the faithful: "Pray brethren that my sacrifice and yours may be accepted by God the almighty Father" (*Orate Fratres*). This and other liturgical texts isolate the dedication of the believing community to the Father too much and so incline to make it too independent of Christ's sacrifice. Catholic reflection on our faith demands a reorientation on the basis of the biblical concept that we only sacrifice by remembering the saving deeds of Christ. This is the only way in which we can sacrifice at all: "Therefore, O Lord, we, your servants and holy people, commemorate the holy suffering, as well as the resurrection from the dead and the glorious ascension into heaven of the same Christ, your Son, our Lord. And from these your own gifts and presents we offer your great majesty this pure sacrifice" (prayer after the consecration). We sacrifice by the objective commemoration of the whole event of salvation. It is this *memoria,* this commemoration which is the act of sacrifice. The Lord offers himself in the action he has told us to perform. When we commemorate the saving deeds of his historic life in the sign of our communion at the eucharistic table, the real importance does not lie in what *we* do but in what his Spirit does in us. We come to this communion with empty hands, and while not merely passive, we do nothing but receive.

This ecumenical approach to the way we confess the eucharist, which there is no room here to develop any further, demands certain applications in those situations where local Roman Catholic Churches and the Churches of the Reformation have already achieved a genuine living together and cooperation. The pluriformity already recognized by Vatican Council II must leave these local Churches the freedom to take such decisions on their own responsibility. It is not realistic to demand of the whole Church a maximum speed of ecumenical development, but one may ask at least a minimum speed of all the local Churches. Otherwise we shall be hampered by stoppages and clashes.

Walter Abbott, S.J./*Chestnut Hill, Massachusetts*

# Common Ecumenical Work for the Bible

During the decade before Vatican Council II, the possibility of a common Bible text and common translations gradually became known among leaders of the Christian Churches. Catholic and Protestant scholars had long known of it, especially since 1943, when, in the encyclical *Divino Afflante Spirito,* Pope Pius XII encouraged Catholic scholars to take advantage of every advance in historical, archeological and linguistic studies to find the sense originally intended by the biblical authors. The sharing of an immense amount of excellent, objective work on both sides resulted in Catholics and Protestants contributing to each other's scholarly journals, studying at each other's centers, attending each other's scholarly meetings and working together on archeological excavations. Collaboration in the work on the Dead Sea Scrolls was especially helpful in showing how much could be done by dedicated, objective men of different denominations.

## The New Policy of the Catholic Church

By 1958, some biblical scholars were seeing this scholarly communication as a step toward Christian unity. Father Alexander Jones of England (already at work on the English edition of the *Bible de Jerusalem* that he would bring out in 1966) told an audience in Sydney, Australia, that the Bible could lead to a "possible rapprochement or even union between the Christian

26

Churches". That same year, Father Robert North, S.J., of the Pontifical Biblical Institute, said in Ottawa that interest in biblical studies was uniting Christians and was an indirect "formula of unity" for the Church. An Episcopalian scholar, Dr. Robert C. Dentan, addressing the Catholic Biblical Association of America at its annual meeting, stressed common interest in the Bible as a source of unity.[1]

By the time of Vatican Council II it was evident to many others what potential for Christian unity there was in a common Bible. There were difficulties to be encountered, of course. Most Protestants did not accept the deutero-canonical books as belonging to the canonical scriptures; Catholic and Protestant missionaries had developed different vocabularies for theological terms in the Bible; Catholics and Protestants had quite different views about notes accompanying the Bible. It was encouraging, however, that more and more Catholic and Protestant leaders approached the difficulties in a spirit of willingness to overcome them rather than to be overcome by them.

Thus, in June, 1964, at Driebergen in Holland, a conference of leaders of the United Bible Societies and delegates of Protestant Churches together with guests from the Catholic Church noted that all Christians are called "to accept a common responsibility for making it possible for all men to have, understand and believe the scriptures", and recommended that there should be "preparation, in collaboration with all Churches, including the Roman Catholic Church, of a common text in the original languages, to be the one source of translation for all Christians". The conference stated the conviction that "by means of honest scholarship this is now a possibility", and it encouraged "the exploration of the possibility of preparing, at least in certain languages, a common translation of the Bible that may be published either in common or separately as circumstances may require".[2]

---

[1] Cf. W. M. Abbott, S.J., "The Bible Is a Bond," in *America* (Oct. 24, 1959), pp. 100-02.
[2] For the full text of the Conference message, cf. *United Bible Societies Bulletin*, No. 60 (Fourth Quarter, 1964), pp. 181-83.

On a number of occasions, officials of the Bible Societies have stressed that their organizations are not formally engaged in the ecumenical movement and that their work is simply what it has always been: providing the Word of God in each man's language at a price he can afford to pay. In seeking the ever wider distribution of the scriptures, the Bible Societies serve all Churches and communities. However, since the Bible has become a "precious instrument" [3] for the work of ecumenism, promoters of Bible translation and distribution, whatever their immediate objectives may be, do in fact become precious instruments themselves in "the mighty hand of God" [4] for the work of Christian unity. Leaders of the Bible Societies rightly point out to constituencies not interested in, or even fearful of, ecumenism that what the Churches and individuals do with the scriptures provided by the Societies is something beyond the purposes and the control of the Societies, but whatever it is, it should not impede the ever wider circulation of the scriptures.[5]

In the spirit of willingness to overcome difficulties rather than to be overcome by them, Pope Paul VI and the Catholic bishops of the world made this statement of policy on November 18, 1965: "Easy access to Sacred Scripture should be provided for all the Christian faithful. . . . And if, given the opportunity and the approval of Church authority, these translations are pro-

[3] *Decree on Ecumenism*, n. 21.

[4] *Ibid.*

[5] Bishop J. G. M. Willebrands, Secretary of the Vatican Secretariat for Promoting Christian Unity, in addressing a meeting of the United Bible Societies Executive Committee, London, January 10, 1968, stated: "We know that the Bible Societies as such are not engaged in ecumenism but are solely concerned with the spread of the scriptures for evangelism. Like many other Churches, the Roman Catholic Church is concerned with both ecumenism and evangelism. This fact does not prevent you from cooperating with these Churches as well as others that have little or no concern for ecumenism, because you are careful to make clear that you focus entirely on your work of producing scriptures for evangelism, and the Churches know you leave all other matters and concerns to them. As a result of this policy, the Bible Societies, in many cases, have on their boards and national advisory councils representatives of twice as many Churches as the national or regional councils of Churches, which are formally at work in the field of ecumenism" (*SPCU Information Service*, No. 4, March, 1968, p. 8.

duced in cooperation with the separated brethren as well, all Christians will be able to use them." [6] This endorsement in principle of the common Bible and of collaboration in translation was followed by the urging of collaboration in distribution of the Bible: "Editions of the sacred scriptures, provided with suitable comments, should be prepared also for the use of non-Christians and adapted to their situation. . . . Both pastors of souls and Christians generally should see to the wise distribution of these in one way or another." [7]

## The Result of Cooperation

The new policy of the Catholic Church brought a warm response from the Bible Societies. At its 1966 meeting, the UBS Council voted unanimously to cooperate with Roman Catholics wherever possible. Subsequent continental meetings of the Bible Societies and delegates from the Churches already collaborating with them passed similar votes.[8] On January 5, 1967 a meeting of translation experts from the Bible Societies and Catholic scholars in Rome drew up the final draft of guiding principles for interconfessional cooperation in translating the Bible. In his opening address to the group, Cardinal Bea said: "It does not seem to be an exaggeration to say that the possibility of our cooperation is one of the most important developments in con-

---

[6] *Dogmatic Constitution on Divine Revelation*, n. 22.

[7] *Ibid.*, n. 25. The *Constitution on Divine Revelation* did not have cooperation in translation and distribution as its main object, but when the idea of a common Bible and common Bible translations matured in the Council and the time came for it to be put into a document somewhere, it ended up in this Constitution because it dealt with the Bible. Thus a document that was concerned with internal renewal of the Catholic Church contains an addition that goes beyond internal affairs—a return to the Bible for Catholics.

[8] The UBS Council met at Buck Hill Falls, Pennsylvania, in May, 1966. The continental meeting for Africa took place at Winneba, Ghana, in March, 1967; for Europe, at St. Cergue, Switzerland, September, 1967; for Asia, at Bangkok, Thailand, November, 1967; for the Americas, at Oaxtepec, Mexico, December, 1968. Reports are given in each case in the subsequent issues of the *United Bible Societies Bulletin* (101 Queen Victoria St., London EC 4, England) and the Information Service of the Secretariat for Promoting Christian Unity (Via dell' Erba, 1—00193 Rome, Italy).

temporary Christian history." The document of guiding principles, including solutions to such problems as the handling of
deutero-canonical books and annotations, was published on
Pentecost Sunday, June 2, 1968.[9] During the preceding months,
the UBS member societies had ratified the executive committee's
approval, and all proper steps had been taken at the Vatican in
preparation for the joint publication of the document. In the
meantime it had also been agreed that Father Carlo M. Martini,
S.J., of the Pontifical Biblical Institute, would join the four Protestants who formed the editorial committee for the edition of the
Greek New Testament adopted as the basis for common translation work; Father Norbert Lohfink, S.J., also of the Pontifical
Biblical Institute, had been added to the Bible Societies group
working on a new edition of Kittel's Hebrew Old Testament text;
Catholics had been added to several dozen teams of translators at
work in African and Asian languages; one common Bible translation project had begun to publish its work.[10]

The result of cooperation, the result of earnest and honest
effort to produce accurate translations together, can be the providing of low-cost New Testaments and eventually complete Bi-
bles for millions of people throughout the world who would
otherwise not have a copy of the scriptures in their hands. Thus
the purpose of the Bible Societies will be better fulfilled, and the
people involved in the translating and distributing of the Bible
will also *de facto* have a share in the work of ecumenism.

The immense increase in Bible distribution that can result
from such cooperation will have another result that is important
for the work of ecumenism: people everywhere will need, and
want, courses of instruction in the Bible, low-cost booklets and
pamphlets that will guide them through the sacred books. Bish-

[9] For the text, cf. *SPCU Information Service,* No. 5, June, 1968, pp.
22-25, and the commentary article in the same issue, pp. 13-20. Text and
commentary article were published also in *La Documentation Catholique,*
No. 1518 (June 2, 1968), pp. 981-1008. The text is also available in
German, Italian and Spanish at the SPCU office in Rome.

[10] *Traduction oecumenique de la Bible: Epître de Saint Paul aux Ro-
mains,* co-published by L'Alliance biblique universelle and Les Editions
du Cerf, Paris, France (January, 1967).

ops and priests will be called upon to give more of their time to teaching and discussing the Bible. All this will help to achieve the pastoral aims of Vatican Council II's *Constitution on Divine Revelation*. At the same time, it will draw bishops and priests more directly into the work of ecumenism, because the increase of Bible reading among Catholics will encourage Protestants and Orthodox, in the spirit of the times, to make inquiries about what the Holy Spirit is doing among their Catholic brethren now drinking deeply from the same sources of inspiration.

## Practical Possibilities

Providentially, an important source of help for Catholic bishops and priests in all this work has been developing in Europe. Quite independently of each other—they had not even met until a conference at Cardinal Bea's Secretariat brought them together April 22-24, 1958—leaders of the Catholic Biblical Associations in Germany and Holland called for an international organization that would enable the Catholic Church to do what Vatican Council II called for in the sixth chapter of the *Constitution on Divine Revelation*. The German Katholisches Bibelwerk especially—a national organization with representatives and dues-paying members in each diocese benefiting from, and providing for others, a complete service of pastoral biblical helps—could be a model for other countries where no Catholic Biblical Association yet exists.[11] At any rate, the members of the existing associations gathered at the conference in Rome regarded the proposed International Catholic Federation for the Biblical Apostolate as a service to the bishops of the world in the task of the hierarchy concerning the promotion, use and understanding of the scriptures among priests and people. They also stated an ecumenical aspect of the proposed federation by declaring that from its very inception such an organization should collaborate as closely as possible with the United Bible Societies.[12] In the

[11] For information, address the Director, Silberburgstrasse 121, 7 Stuttgart W, West Germany.

[12] Cf. Report on the Conference in *SPCU Information Service*, No. 5, June, 1968, pp. 12-13.

course of the conference, the work of the United Bible Societies was clarified as that of translation, production and supply specialists; the Catholic Associations would be most concerned about pastoral care around the Bible—that is, about biblical formation of priests and people, about training of clergy and laity for work in the biblical apostolate.

The bishops of some countries—for example, Germany, Holland and the United States—are fortunate that they and their priests have at hand a whole corps of Catholic men and women who are capable of engaging in dialogue with Protestants. In the United States it is a result of the educational system that the bishops, the religious orders and the people have so heroically built up. Because so many men and women are graduates of Catholic colleges and universities where they had good courses in Scripture and theology, especially in the period after World War II, the call went out to the National Council of Catholic Men and the National Council of Catholic Women to take greater part in the dialogue. In 1963 the national convention of the National Catholic Educational Association had for its theme "Fostering the Ecumenical Spirit". With the encouragement of the bishops who are moderators of the three associations, the NCCM, the NCCW, and the NCEA are providing helps of all kinds to those among the laity who have the interest and ability for ecumenical dialogue, especially the dialogue on basic teachings of the Bible.

The future of ecumenism in the United States is particularly bright because practically all Catholic colleges and universities have put good Scripture courses into the required curriculum, and, in accordance with the directives of Vatican Council II, the biblical approach has spread throughout the high school and elementary levels. The day may soon come when Catholics rather generally will match the traditional zeal of Protestants for Bible study in their schools and in all forms of their lay apostolate.

For sustaining the good biblical work begun in the schools and constantly being improved at college level, the Christian Family Movement stands out among the laity. In the Chicago area, where it began, there are more than 17,000 active couples in this Catholic movement. Throughout the United States there are more than 100,000 couples holding regular CFM meetings. This means that more than 200,000 Catholic men and women—most of them college or university graduates—regularly study the scriptures, since, according to CFM rules, the first fifteen minutes of every meeting are devoted to biblical study and discussion. CFM meetings are held every two weeks; a meeting involves from four to seven couples who have banded together for programs that are planned out over a year; one couple will serve as leaders of the group. All the leaders of a parish area will meet beforehand with a priest to get guidance from him. A CFM group could be called, therefore, a kind of scriptural cell.

Since CFM people are often college or university professors of literature, history and other humanistic studies calling for some acquaintance with Scripture, as well as lawyers, doctors, editors and professional people accustomed to some kind of research, their meeting with the priest requires him to give the best possible fruits of his own study of the scriptures. In addition to the direction of the priest, CFM couples have a flow of good, new commentaries and books on Scripture to nourish the life of their cell. Young Catholic college graduates in the suburbs are the backbone of the CFM movement. They are not far away from their Scripture and theology courses. If they feel a bit rusty, they can turn to the fourteen booklets of the New Testament Reading Guide published by the Liturgical Press [13] and the continuation of the series through the Old Testament, or they can turn to the series published by Paulist Press.[14]

The CFM people are probably the best among the hundreds of thousands at work in the Confraternity of Christian Doctrine throughout the United States, especially in giving weekly instruction to Catholic students attending non-Catholic schools. The CCD also has a program for reaching non-Catholics, as well as an office for closer cooperation between the CCD program and

[13] Liturgical Press, Collegeville, Minn., U.S.A.
[14] Paulist Press, 304 W. 58th St., New York, N.Y.

efforts of ecumenical groups. In some American cities and suburbs, with the approval of pastors and cooperation of priests,
Catholic and Protestant couples meet for ecumenical Bible study
sessions that are like the first fifteen minutes of a CFM meeting.
It is only one step beyond the reading of the Bible together such
as has become common during Church Unity Week services. It is
a step, however, that involves much more, and therefore the best
qualified people are required in order that the work may proceed
properly and profitably.

Another source of help for bishops and priests who will need
assistance in handling the demand for guidance in reading the
Bible is to be found among the secular institutes. The two dozen
secular institutes in the United States do not yet have a membership the size of the Christian Family Movement, but these totally
dedicated people are studying Scripture with the zeal they give to
chosen projects. An example of what they can do comes from
California, where some men in a parish asked members of a
secular institute for women to promote a weekend discussion
on the passion of our Lord. Thirty-eight people came for the two
days, practically filling the house and chapel of the secular institute. There were four priests from four different orders, four
religious sisters from three different communities and four students; the rest were men and women from the local parish. After
the four priests concelebrated Mass on Saturday morning, discussion centered around the scriptural accounts of the passion;
in the afternoon, the sacramental aspects were discussed. To give
the discussion an historical flavor, an authentic Seder supper was
held, with the prior of a nearby Benedictine monastery taking
the role of father of the family; they had all the ceremonial foods
and drink, with a typical Jewish family meal; the questions of the
Haggadah were asked by a teenaged daughter of one of the parishioners. The meaning of the ceremony was explained in a short
rehearsal, and the guests were also taught the Hebrew songs for
this night, which were then "sung with gusto by all at certain
peak intermissions", as the newsletter of the secular institute
later reported. On Sunday morning a priest sang the liturgy of St.

John Chrysostom. Sunday afternoon was devoted to discussion of personal, ascetical answers to our Lord's passion.

It would take only a little imagination, and the zeal that comes from the Holy Spirit, to see how this kind of program could become ecumenical in its makeup. It takes intelligent, dedicated, talented people to manage that kind of program. It takes people who know the doctrine of their Church and how to preserve it in its purity. The secular institutes have such people, and they are eager to serve.

In addition to the clergy and well-educated laity, the bishops have to think of all the faithful entrusted to them and give them "suitable instruction in the right use of the divine books, especially the New Testament and above all the gospels" through versions that are provided with "necessary and fully adequate explanations so that the sons of the Church can safely and profitably grow familiar with the sacred scriptures and be penetrated with their spirit".[15] Many of the people will want more than this minimum. The archdiocese of Montreal, Canada, has developed something worthy of imitation everywhere: an archdiocesan Bible centre that publishes a weekly six-page leaflet entitled "I Discover the Bible".[16] The leaflet synchronizes study of the Bible with the liturgical cycle, and it is available in all churches of the archdiocese. A great amount of sound knowledge and considerable communication of the spirit of the scriptures are achieved in the course of a year through use of the leaflet. Again, it takes only a little imagination to see how this kind of instrument could be used for a rather wide circle of people who want to do some work for ecumenism.[17]

[15] *Dogmatic Constitution on Divine Revelation*, n. 25.

[16] There is also a French edition of the leaflet "Le Feuillet Biblique." Both editions come from The Bible Centre, 2000 Sherbrooke Street West, Montreal 25, Canada.

[17] The Daughters of St. Paul are developing an international ecumenical correspondence course (Centro Ut Unum Sint, Via Antonino Pio, 75—00145, Rome, Italy), and the cardinal archbishop of Westminster has approved Catholic participation in the Bible Reading Fellowship, whose notes for Bible study, now prepared by an ecumenical group, are read by some 400,000 people throughout the world (148 Buckingham Palace Road, London, S.W. 1, England).

Vatican Council II's *Decree on Ecumenism* calls all Catholics to ecumenical work according to their ability. As Cardinal Bea said, on a visit to the United States in 1965, the great task of the Church in the immediate future is to see that Vatican Council II's *Decree on Ecumenism* does not become the privilege of "an elect few". The Decree, he pointed out, calls for a mobilization of the Church down to her last member in the work of Christian unity. How this is to be done is being spelled out gradually by competent authorities—the Holy See, episcopal conferences and local ordinaries—but it has been self-evident from the beginning of the Church's interest in the work of ecumenism that an appropriate knowledge of the Bible is necessary at each level of the work. Acquaintance with truly objective work, communicated in such leaflets as those published by the Montreal Bible Center, will protect the people from false efforts when they discuss the Bible with their friends and by this means try to make some contribution to Christian unity. Teachers of religion, of course, at all levels—from early catechism through college theology courses—have an obligation to acquaint themselves with the best work that is being done on the Bible in order to communicate it to their students for the use they can later make of it in their dialogues with neighbors who, like themselves, will want to do more than build a new home, raise a family and live the good life.

In giving so much attention to the Bible and to biblical themes, we do not mean to suggest that Scripture should be treated without consulting tradition. In fact, the more that Catholics and other Christians can communicate with each other from the sound teachings and explanations of the Christian faith in their traditions, the better the ecumenical movement will be. We wish to stress here simply that a common understanding of the scriptural meaning that God gave us is essential if we are to pray intelligently with the Church and find ourselves ultimately together again in the same fold about which the Good Shepherd spoke.

Jos Lescrauwaet, M.S.C./*Tilburg, Netherlands*

# Ecumenical Corrections in Our Preaching

First of all, let us be clear about the fact that ecumenical corrections in the presentation of our faith can only be effective when handled by a preacher, lecturer or author who has a genuine ecumenical mentality. The corrections indeed concern facts that can be pointed to, but no fact is so objective that it cannot be subjectively slanted by whoever mentions it: the tone and accent will always be his own, he will always place it in the context with which he is familiar, and so it will always be accompanied by connotations that are peculiarly his own.

## The Ecumenical Attitude

The preacher or lecturer must personally be profoundly aware of what binds separated Christians together. This common element lies at a level which is deeper than that of what makes them differ from each other. And here it is not only a matter of doctrinal agreement but primarily of the saving reality of sharing in the life of Jesus Christ. All Christians have access to their creator as their Father, and this Father is one and the same for all. All Christians share in a brotherhood with Christ and therefore with each other, for Christ is one and the same for all. All Christians experience this living reality in virtue of an indivisible Spirit of whom they can say "Abba" and "Jesus is the Lord".

This factual experience and primary witness gave rise to the apostolic confession of faith born at the baptismal celebration in Jerusalem, the mother community of all Churches. This confession of the one believing community, like the reality of the one baptism, is more powerful than we usually realize after all the centuries of inter-Christian controversies. The reference to the apostolic creed of the baptismal home of Jerusalem should not lead us to think that Chrisians are only linked with each other by their origin. The reality, created by the one baptism and the one basic apostolic confession, still forges a unity now, right through the walls that separate the various denominations. Moreover, this one baptism and this one confession imply an actual and common mission. We all leave the baptismal home with the common mission to tell all men what God has planned in his love for mankind in the present and the future. Today nobody will have to point out how extremely urgent this proclamation of the apostolic witness is; it is the decisive condition to fulfill Christ's mandate "that the world may believe".

In pre-ecumenical times the attitude was mainly determined by an otherwise believing consciousness of what distinguished each Church or ecclesial community. It implicitly pointed to the boundaries marked out by inter-Christian controversies. The ecumenical attitude does not necessarily deny the specific characteristics of a given Church, but it is aware of the relative character of these features over against what we have basically in common. It also knows that this foundation is the central point which supports the whole Christian mansion with its separate living rooms and that it extends far beyond what was realized by the inhabitants of the isolated "flats".

The ecumenical mentality also differs from the apologetic one by an atmosphere of modesty. How relative specific opinions and practices are stands out more sharply not only against the background of what we have basically and centrally in common but also against the typical features of the other Churches when we compare them with our own. The point here is not less appreciation of one's own traditions but rather less pretentiousness. No single theological system is exhaustive and complete, no single doctrinal proposition is the last and definitive one, no single community structure is the ultimate one. This relativity does not deny the truth or goodness of a system, a formula or a structure, but reduces it to the proportions of human abilities, no doubt guided by the Spirit but essentially limited all the same. The admission that, after all, we are only human means that the faithful, too, should always reckon with the reality of sin, which impairs our resolutions and blurs our insights.

Inspired by awareness of this limitation, Vatican Council II laid down the following directive: "Catholic theologians engaged in ecumenical dialogue, while standing fast by the teaching of the Church and searching together with the separated brethren into the divine mysteries, should act with love for truth, with charity and with humility" (*Decree on Ecumenism*, n. 11).

Finally, the ecumenical mentality is marked by hopefulness for the future. We shall overcome our divisions. Made wiser by the conflicts and the process of reconciliation, we shall become better equipped to establish the validity of the Gospel's call for the whole inhabited world. After so many controversies, that original Christian force must again be set free so that it can gather all men around the one source of true and lasting life for their own fully human fulfillment. Connan has described this force when he said that this ecumenism is "the dynamism which operates unceasingly in order to win the world and to change it according to the Gospel".[1] A preacher or catechist who allows this force to work within himself knows spontaneously what is basically common to and what is valuable but relative in all Christian communities. He can and will apply the corrections, suggested below, according to their value.

### Corrections of a General Nature

Catechisms have been used since the 16th century. The polemic and simplifying character of this kind of popular instruction

---

[1] G. Connan, *Le rôle des Pères dans l'élaboration de l'œcuménisme chrétien* (Berlin, 1959), p. 157.

is no cause for astonishment. Controversy, however, concentrates on articles of faith that are thought to be threatened. This leads to a narrowing of views that overlook the proportions contained in the wider context and creates blind spots which prevent any possible development. The simplified formulation of the faith in the form of question and answer is bound to lead to a "black-and-white" judgment, expressed in a simple yes or no. I give examples in the next paragraph, but we can already see in general that some formulas of faith are put into such contrasts that they lose in fullness and balance. In the same way, points attacked either by the Eastern or the Protestant Churches were so heavily and prominently stressed in the Catholic interpretation that the overall picture of Catholicism showed definite contortions.

We must also mend our use of words. Every Christian tradition developed in its separate existence a certain individual use of language—sometimes special words, or words with their own peculiar connotation, sometimes covering presuppositions, left unspoken, but by no means obvious to others. The word "rite" means for the Latin Catholic the outward shape of worship, for an Eastern Christian it means both worship and the structure of an ecclesial community and usually also the national character of a given local Church, while for Protestants the word is associated with purely external gestures. Words that have a different sound for Catholics and Protestants are, for instance, grace and merit, sacrament as sign and as operative, altar and sacrifice, office and ministry, holy and sinful, not to mention the misunderstandings about priestly power and the infallibility of pope or Church. The ecumenical attitude is on the lookout for terms that are clear and can easily be understood by everyone, so that listeners can grasp what we really mean.

Finally, our preaching must learn to apply the conciliar thought that "in Catholic teaching there exists an order or 'hierarchy' of truths, since they vary in their relation to the foundation of the Christian faith" (*Decree on Ecumenism*, n. 11). In the past, theology was already aware of the distinction between truths deemed necessary for salvation and other truths described as most useful. Even most catechisms acknowledge a list of four "principal truths" concerning the reality of God, the incarnation of God's Son, the mediation of Jesus Christ through his death on the cross, and the last judgment of ourselves as good or evil. Here one usually referred to Hebrews 11, 6: "Anyone who comes to God must believe that he exists and rewards those who try to find him," and to John 17, 3: "And eternal life is this: to know you, the only true God, and Jesus Christ whom you have sent." On the basis of this distinction between the truths of faith, Bishop A. Pangrazio led the Council to a new application of it and distinguished between "revealed truths which express the mystery of Christ and truths of ecclesial elements that build up the Church". In his explanation he spoke about "truths that belong to the aim, such as the mystery of the Trinity, the incarnation of the Word and redemption, the love of God and his grace with regard to sinful mankind, eternal life in the fulfillment of the kingdom" and "truths that belong to the means of salvation, such as the seven sacraments, the hierarchical structure of the Church, apostolic succession and similar ones". He then observed that the doctrinal differences between Christians mainly concern the second category of truths, and "that all Christians are one in the matter of the primary truths of the Christian religion".[2] The importance of this view for preaching is obvious. It does not mean that Catholic secondary truths are denied, but that they are not treated as belonging to the same level as the Apostles' Creed, that they should not be allowed to dominate the whole Catholic presentation of the faith, and that one may wonder whether certain truths should still be considered as justifying a division in the Church. From the ecumenical point of view, this third correction is probably the most important.[3]

[2] *Council Speeches of Vatican II*, ed. by Y. Congar, H. Küng, and D. O'Hanlon (London, 1965).

[3] H. Mühler, "Die Lehre Vaticanum II über die Hierarchia veritatum," in *Theologie und Glaube* 57 (1966), pp. 303-35.

## Some Concrete Corrections

The application of all that has been said concerns, first of all, our public worship and particularly that of every Sunday where more attention must be given to the service of the Word. The influence of constantly repeated preaching, the prayers and hymns is more important than the explicit mention of one-sided slogans of the Counter-Reformation and aspects of faith that have been neglected by us and better preserved by the Reformed Churches. That is why the ecumenical mentality of the pastor is of primary importance, so that he can stress new points intelligently and spontaneously.

In the celebration of the sacraments it should become much clearer than in the past that sacraments are a matter of actions of faith, where the personal commitment to faith is not the only but certainly an essential factor in the effectiveness of the sign through which Christ wants to work his salvation. The function of the Word within the sacramental action must emerge as decisive; it is the Word which lifts the action out of its natural multiplicity of meaning to the level of Christ's own meaning and appeals directly to the actual act of faith in which he communicates himself to us. Thus we can correct the one-sidedness and usually misunderstood meaning of the expression "ex opere operato".

The universal priesthood of all those who are baptized should not be "taught" so much as gradually put into practice. Parishioners will realize that Christian community life in a given locality stands or falls with the effective sense of responsiblity of all to the extent that they are actively involved in the liturgical and other ecclesial gatherings. This will show at the same time that the proper function of a priesthood as service consists in a "service to unity" both in the local community and, via the bishop, in the whole Church. This practical realization of the universal priesthood will put the special priesthood in its proper context.

When the parish begins to realize that it is held together by the unifying power of the Spirit of the Lord who, by means of

Christ's Word and sacrament, creates harmony and unity in prayer, witness and care for each other and for all men, then it will also know that Church government does not create the Church's unity but serves it. Living out in faith the reality of baptism and the eucharist with all their social implications manifests and brings about unity in Christ. Aimed at this unity, so powerfully compared by Scripture with that of the human body, the services operate in such a way "that there may not be disagreements inside the body but that each part may be equally concerned for all the others" (1 Cor. 12, 25). This helps to correct our view of the primacy of Peter, which is not the source of Christian unity but the instrument which must be an aid toward unity.

The manner of the eucharistic celebration must show that the choice between meal and sacrifice damages the integrity of this mystery. As a meal it establishes our communion with the unique and unrepeatable self-sacrifice of the Lord in the present. Then, we should not attempt to answer the question "how" the Lord is present without considering the whole purpose of this presence. In the confusion of its age, the Council of Trent did not provide an exhaustive explanation of the mystery of the eucharist, but picked only two acute problems out of the whole complex and formulated the Catholic interpretation of these two problems—namely, the real presence of the Lord and the sacrifical character of the celebration. Post-Tridentine preaching used these two statements exclusively as the basic pattern to serve the polemical situation. And here the catechism of the Counter-Reformation still forgot that the Council of Trent nevertheless speaks of "the Lord's supper" with "food and drink", of "sacramental representation" and of "the unity of the mystical body" as the purpose of the eucharistic celebration. We can correct the traditional view ecumenically when we do not start from the real or supposed Protestant view but from the data of the Bible and the early Church. This is already applied in theology and catechetics, but the liturgical application in rite and word still needs working out, and this is the most important application, given the nature of this mystery, while it is at the same time the most influential in giving practical guidance to ordinary church-goers.

In Catholic preaching Mary occupies an important place, and this is seen as typically Catholic. It would definitely not be an ecumenical correction henceforward to say nothing or little about the mother of the Lord, since Mary has an important place of her own in the Gospel and a unique position in the Church. These two points show, however, which way the ecumenical correction should go. Hence, Vatican Council II did not deal with Mary in a separate document, but rather in a chapter on "the Blessed Virgin Mary, Mother of God, in the mystery of Christ and the Church" (cf. Chapter VIII of the *Constitution on the Church*). To isolate the mother of the Lord from the work of Christ and from that of the Church as the community of those who believe in Christ would be contrary to the Gospel and our ecumenical mission.

*Conclusion*

There are still other points that need to be corrected in an ecumenical sense in our preaching. There are, for instance, points of Church history such as the question of responsibility for the schism between East and West, the real intent of the Reformation and Catholic reaction to it, and others. On this point, the *Decree on Ecumenism* says: "Instruction in sacred theology and other branches of knowledge, especially those of an historical nature, must also be presented from an ecumenical point of view, so that at every point they may more accurately correspond with the facts of the case" (n. 10). A sound and informed revision "worked out in this spirit and not polemically" (*ibid.*) is urgent. But just as important is the way in which priests and teachers convey this information in their work. Here a provocative way of contrasting what was said then with what we preach now is of little use and often partially untrue. With a believing understanding of the basic pattern of the Christian proclamation, the primary articles of faith and the main lines of salvation history, the correction will come about spontaneously in most cases. People will not be easily "shocked" when one puts one-sided statements in their context by supplying the missing elements and guides people back to the heart of Christian witness. Finally, the indirect "preaching" in the way the sacraments are celebrated and the community is experienced will certainly contribute as much to ecumenical formation as direct instruction, because of the instructive character of seeing and doing and the development of an ecumenical mentality, attitude and receptivity. And here we are back where we started: this mentality underlies and is the aim of all possible corrections.

Martin Reardon/*Sheffield, England*

# Ecumenism in the Parish

Ecumenism, like catholicity, has a qualitative as well as a quantitative aspect. It is an attitude of humble dependence upon God, of love of one's fellow Christians and of concern for the world at large, and this attitude will be the same everywhere, however many or few Christians of other traditions one may meet. Its procedures, however, will be different from place to place and no detailed guidance can apply universally.

## Different Situations

1. There are still many parishes in the world (though with rapid communications these are decreasing) where all the Christians belong to one communion. Ecumenism there will include learning from all sources about other traditions in a spirit of self-criticism and of informed prayer for Christians all over the world.

2. In an increasing number of places, even where there is only one organized church, there are individual Christians of other traditions. Ecumenism here will raise the question of how far these individuals can be incorporated into the life of the local Church without losing their attachment to their own denomination and without losing the gifts of their particular tradition. Each situation is likely to be different, and so generalizations are

46

dangerous. One point, however, needs to be made. The special contributions of a few individuals of one communion can easily be dissipated unless they are at least occasionally encouraged and helped to meet and worship in their own tradition. It may therefore be the ecumenical duty of a majority Church in this situation to give the few individuals of another tradition in their midst the facilities for meeting and worshiping as a group in order that they may retain their own particular witness.

3. In many areas of the world there are Churches of only two traditions, usually Roman Catholic and Protestant or Catholic and Orthodox. It is often here that the hostility has been most marked in the past and the initiation of ecumenism is therefore most difficult now. On the other hand, it is often here that the practical opportunities are greatest. In learning about another tradition, there is no substitute for meeting and cooperating with practicing representatives of that tradition.

4. Where there are Churches of more than two different traditions, as is increasingly the case in towns and cities all over the world, practical problems begin to multiply. Very often the parish boundaries of the different denominations do not coincide and a decision has to be made about who cooperates with whom. Time becomes a problem. Each Church has its own list of activities and it becomes increasingly difficult to find suitable times for joint study, prayer or action. On the other hand, the advantage of having at least three traditions meeting together is that in any head-on collision between two, there is usually a third which can act as an interpreter and reconciler.

In an article of this scope it is obviously impossible to deal at all adequately with each of these four situations. Moreover conditions vary from country to country. It is only fair therefore to state that the writer's experience has been gained chiefly in an English city.

## Tensions

The original impetus for the ecumenical movement came from missionaries and students. The leadership then passed to theologians and Church leaders. In some places they have succeeded so well that local Churches are now pestering their leaders to allow them to proceed faster along the road to unity. A twofold tension has resulted. On the one hand, the leaders have found themselves in the familiar role of maintainers of unity, being torn both ways by their flocks, some wanting to move faster and some more slowly toward reunion. On the other hand, it is becoming clear that the primary problems or pressures for unity facing the leaders and theologians are by no means the same as the problems and pressures at work in the local situation, and the significance of this tension has not yet been fully appreciated. It is no longer a tension between those in favor of ecumenism and those who are not, but a tension between those who wish to foster ecumenism in one way and those who wish to foster it in another way.

Generally, Church leaders encourage local congregations to cooperate in social matters, to pray for unity and to study simplified explanations of the theological problems in the way of unity. In some areas of the world, economic pressures also compel them to recommend joint use of church buildings, etc. (in England the law is being changed in order to facilitate this). At the parish level the pressures and problems are often quite different. The theological presentations of the leaders are often misunderstood or ignored. One of the main difficulties that those proposing a scheme for Anglican-Methodist reunion in Britain had to overcome was the reconciliation of episcopal and non-episcopal ministries. Yet after one whole evening devoted to an explanation of this problem and the proposed solution, the only response from a meeting of neighboring Anglican and Methodist congregations was: "It's a pity that our ministers are not more charitable to one another!"

There has been growing pressure from local congregations for mutual sharing in the sacraments at a relatively early stage of ecumenical contact, even where (as in the Anglican and Roman Catholic Churches) the leaders have discouraged this. On the other hand, suggestions from the leaders that social groups amalgamate and forego their identity (e.g., women's groups) are often met with violent opposition, for it is often in these groups that a sense of fellowship and belonging is strongest and members fear losing this support in amalgamation with an unfamiliar group. The joint use of premises and the closing of a familiar church building often provokes this response to an extreme degree: "My father and grandfather worshiped in this building, and I would rather die than leave it."

In these tensions it is wrong to conclude that the leaders are trying to overcome the theological problems and that the local congregations are enmeshed in non-theological factors. Certainly the leaders will have more theological education and therefore will be able to present a more unified theological position. Nevertheless, it is important to realize that the leaders are also reacting to sociological pressures and that it is their role to maintain denominational unity. They are therefore committed to the maintenance of order in the Church. This does not mean that Canon Law cannot change, but it is untidy and difficult for them if it does not change everywhere at the same time. Their position in the Church makes it easier for them to understand the universal geographical aspects of catholicity and ecumenism (of unity) than its local expression and implications. They need to be reminded that the word "ecclesia" in the New Testament is used primarily, if not exclusively, of the local Church, and never simply of a universal *geographical* entity—of the sum of all Christians alive at this moment in this world. Unity in the New Testament is seen primarily as a mystical thing and its canonical implications are only subsidiary. In the New Testament the two poles of unity are seen as the gathering of baptized believers in a locality, and the universal unity of all Christians of all *ages* and places. For this reason one could argue that the unity of the baptized believers gathering in one place is of more ultimate significance than the organizational unity of all Christians alive *at one time* on this planet.

One important conclusion of this observation is the urgent need for qualified theologians to steep themselves in the pressures and problems of local work for unity. So far most theology of ecumenism has been written from the universal point of view. This needs now to be complemented from the local point of view. As this begins to happen, one discovers that many of the cries of the local congregation have considerable theological justification. To take one single example; at the Third Assembly of the World Council of Churches in New Delhi in 1961, the Anglican Church of India, Pakistan, Burma and Ceylon invited all the delegates to receive communion together. "Why," asked an Anglican vicar in England, "do the leaders of our Churches allow themselves intercommunion when they meet together only once every seven years, whereas we are not allowed intercommunion with our neighboring Free Church even though we live and work closely with its members week by week?"

## Future Developments

Let us then look at the forms local ecumenism takes now, estimate the way it may develop in the future, and see some of the theological questions these raise. A recent survey of ecumenical activity in the industrial city of Sheffield in England showed that among some 200 local Churches there were only about 10 parish group meetings which were *regularly* run jointly by members of more than one denomination. (A single local Church might run as many as a dozen different group meetings for old people, young people or men and women each week, so that one could say that only 0.1% of all such meetings are regularly interdenominational.) Only two church buildings were regularly used by congregations of two different denominations, and in one case the two congregations virtually never met each other. Well below 1% of regular Sunday services of worship were joint services in which the members of more than one denomination shared, and scarcely any of these were communion services. About one-seventh of regular Church magazines were published jointly by Churches of different denominations. The only field in which it could ever be claimed that those regularly participating in *joint* activities outnumbered those in activities of one denomination alone was in discussion group meetings in people's homes. For a period of seven weeks in 1967 a nationally sponsored project of interdenominational study and action groups had the participation of more than half the laymen who normally meet in denominational study groups. Apart from this and the number of jointly produced Church magazines, less than 1% of the regular activities of local congregations are shared with congregations of another denomination.

The most popular field for ecumenical activity locally was some special annual occasion. Over half the congregations took part in the annual house-to-house collection organized by the Christian Aid Department of the British Council of Churches. About one third of the congregations held a joint meeting during the Week of Prayer for Christian Unity. About one third shared in some joint effort of social service or evangelism in their neighborhood.

How can the salient features of this survey be summarized? Occasional joint activities (especially those which reach out into the local community), joint meetings in homes and the joint production of magazines met with a far greater response than regular joint activities taking place on church premises. Why is this so? Because the regular activities which have traditionally taken place on church premises in Britain in the last half century have tended to build up supportive groups on church premises in order to help individuals to live Christian lives in their secular surroundings. Any weakening or extending of the local Church group, or any threat to close the premises where the group meets, is therefore a threat to the whole pattern of Christian life. This system militates against any serious ecumenical development. It also has proved singularly ineffective for mission. It is a development of the medieval parochial system. In the Middle Ages in Christendom everyone was nominally Christian, and most people were born, married and died in the same parish. They were educated, worked, spent their leisure and were nursed there. In all this the same parish priest kept track of his flock and searched for the wandering sheep. In a modern town or city he had neither the time nor the means to follow his sheep into the multitude of places where the complicated network of modern life took them, and so he encouraged them to come to a series of different meetings in the fold, hoping by the variety of the meetings to attract as many of the sheep as possible. It was a valiant effort which served its day, but that day has passed.

For this reason, not as serious as it would otherwise have been is the fact that it has proved extremely difficult to persuade local Churches of different traditions to amalgamate the activities normally held on church premises. Local Churches will presumably always gather for worship, but most of these other activities are likely to begin to disappear. Their place will almost certainly be taken by small groups meeting in houses and more flexible institutions of mission in the secular community. We have noted that it is just at these points that ecumenical work is easiest. However, as soon as the local congregations join together for mission in their neighborhood, the nature of that mission is bound to be called into question. There will be those who emphasize evangelism, those who look for increasing church membership and those who believe the call today is for social service or political involvement. There is nothing the ecumenical movement needs more today than a balanced statement of the Church's mission in terms intelligible to the layman. It might perhaps best be debated as an answer to the question: "What is the Church for?" As the answers are given ("a boat to ferry souls to heaven"; "a garage where I come on Sundays to fill up with sufficient spiritual fuel to last me through the week"), it will be seen that those which are least serviceable for mission today are the very ones which do not encourage ecumenism (the more forms of transport to heaven, the more likely everyone is to get there; some people like one brand of petrol, some another). In the parish, as at every other level, mission and unity stand or fall together.

As soon as mission in the parish is taken seriously and a practical, working definition of mission is agreed upon, it should appear that mission today, at least in an industrial society, cannot be confined within parish boundaries. This raises the second question: "What is the local Chruch and what forms should it take?" The medieval concept of the parish as a pastoral unit needs to be augmented by a much more complex concept of pastoral and missionary units which will express the Church's concern for every sector of the secular community. There is likely to be a mission in industry, a mission in education, a mission in the hospital and welfare service, a mission among those sharing a particular leisure activity, a mission in radio and television, and so on. As soon as the Churches move on to these secular preserves, the sin and impossibility of division into different denominations becomes apparent. But how can separate denominations set up united structures of mission until they themselves are fully united? Are controlled experiments feasible where normal rules are broken? [1] How can unity be maintained between the traditional parishes, the new structures of mission, and the wider Church? Such questions need an urgent answer from the theologians.

[1] For a study of experiments in Britain, see R. M. C. Jeffery, *Areas of Ecumenical Experiment* (London, 1968) and his article in the Documentation section of this volume.

John Dillenberger/*Berkeley, California*

# The Integration
# of Theological
# Faculties

A working integration of faculties across denominational and Church boundaries is a very recent development in theological education. For some time there have been individual exchanges or appointments of professors. In Europe Roman Catholic and Protestant faculties occasionally belong to the same universities. But that fact has not guaranteed extensive cooperation in planning programs and facilities. Departments of religion in colleges and universities in the United States have made appointments cutting across the religious spectrum in the search for teachers and scholars qualified in specific subject matter. But inasmuch as American colleges and universities until recently reflected a Protestant establishment, and because Catholic training in religion did not produce the type of scholars desired in secular universities, the number of Catholic scholars so appointed was small. Indeed, Judaic scholars were more adequately represented in the universities, than were Catholics. In Catholic universities, of course, the departments were almost entirely Catholic.

However, even these limited working contracts helped to prepare the soil for more extensive cooperative work. Vatican Council II dramatically extended all such contacts, and in its wake new structures of cooperation were born in many areas of the theological world. In the United States these developments also include the scholarly tradition of Judaism. Concomitant to and in part growing out of Vatican Council II, new conversations arose between the Jewish and Christian communities. These have shifted the nature of the dialogue and in some instances helped to create new structures of cooperative work.

## New Cooperative Structures

It is apparent that there is little experience to draw upon for integrating faculties. Theological faculties, as we know them, did not exist prior to either the Catholic-Protestant split or the internal Protestant splits. Hence, the new possibilities for theological school cooperation have no precedent in history. That is at once a liability and an asset. Unfortunately there is no history of unity which could operate as pressure upon theological faculties. Indeed, theological faculties were largely created to conserve the traditions, not to innovate. Theological faculties were educational agencies designed to safeguard and give protection to the splits within Christendom. This is one of the lingering reasons why ecclesiastics are particularly upset by theological faculties which seem to depart from previously accepted norms.

On the other hand, the lack of a history to which one feels compelled to return, but rather wants to overcome, serves as a partial clearing of the decks. Renewal in that sense can be present- and future-directed. The past is then not a point of return, but a reality into which one enters in order to be instructed for the future.

Given the fact that theological faculties deal with the substance of the faith and that they were formed to elucidate and protect it, the obviously *central issue* in the integration of theological faculties is the problem of whether or not the faith is taught in terms appropriate to the heritage in question. This involves its thought, life and practice—in short, a total orientation. Is it then possible to integrate theological faculties in any form?

The Protestant experience is limited, and when it is applied to wider contexts, it is ambiguous. For much of their history, European theological faculties have been in tension with Church bodies, sometimes because the faculties were so academic in the indifferent sense that the concerns of the Church were not present, and at other times because the Church was not ready for a new, vibrant theological push. Within the United States, Protestant theological schools were divided between denominational schools, usually in isolation, and non-denominational schools formed over against restrictive 19th-century theological positions. By and large the academic standards of the non-denominational schools, until the recent past, were higher than most of the denominational schools. Non-denominational schools supplied many of the faculty even for denominational schools, and were frequently accused of not preparing men for the parish ministry. Nor did students attending such schools, given their mobility, usually return to their own jurisdictions. But in point of fact the non-denominational educational involvement had little effect on Church and denominational allegiances. Most continued to serve the heritage from which they came, though they easily changed allegiances when new positions required it.

Protestant non-denominational schools did reflect a theological direction not acceptable to the more ecclesiastically oriented bodies. The non-denominational faculties represented an orientation more associated with the Free Church tradition than with the traditional Church bodies. While open to all bodies to join them because theological and denominational bodies had little significance, and needed to be overcome, non-denominational faculties had developed no sensitivities for understanding that such a position was offensive to those whose theological position was tied to a strong Church tradition. While the non-denominational approach sidetracked peripheral differences and thereby contributed a new and positive climate, it did not adequately understand confessional and transconfessional issues. Indeed, in our new situation in which ecumenical concerns are so centrally a part of traditional Church schools and bodies, the non-denominational protagonists have not yet come to terms with the new realities. The non-denominational approach is generally not broad enough to encompass and provide equality for all groups, though it invites their presence. Nor is it willing to identify itself with a more sectarian Free Church tradition. While providing a vanguard of experience, non-denominational schools have a more ambiguous and limited role to play than they once did.

The integration of theological faculties requires the full acceptance of diverse orientations, their right to be and to be continued—in short, their structural and functional equality. This may mean different patterns of association and work at various levels of theological education. At the most advanced level—that is, the *doctorate*—single faculty arrangements across the theological spectrum have already shown that the gains are great and that such theological study contributes a breakthrough in scholarship and understanding which are mutually enriching without blurring distinctions. Indeed, precisely this positive experience is fostering the extension of faculty integration in appropriate forms to other levels.

Nevertheless, some have proposed that all theological education be carried out in isolation until the most advanced or doctoral level is reached, for then the basic postures will have been reached. But there is a fallacy in this approach which cuts in two directions. Graduate work, too, may be most fruitful when the theological spectrum is pursued simultaneously, rather than having Protestants, Catholics or Jews simply going to each other's schools. When Catholic seminarians or priests have gone to Protestant schools, leaving their own context behind, there has been just enough incidence of corrosion of their heritage, however temporary, to give ammunition to those seeking it, though to be sure those who so seek will find evidence under any circumstances. But there is a distinct advantage in the integration of faculties insofar as it helps keep all the heritages, including one's own, simultaneously in focus. In that way, research, learning and ways of working are forged in total dialogical contexts.

There is every reason to engage in doctoral work in terms of a total and direct integration of faculties. There is every reason to explore extensive cooperation in the area of continuing education, where basic formation is assumed and where actual ministries do function in relation to each other, from chaplaincies to inner city. Cooperation *at the basic level* of formation for ministries at this juncture of history probably demands another style. Churches and theological institutions will resist cooperative developments which raise questions about the integrity of their own programs. Cooperation which demands major change in institutions is resisted, even if the institutions themselves wish to change on their own.

The psychology of theological training is still far removed from the notion that curriculum, faculty and facilities not only can but ought to work out a *common program*. But major planning and experimental programs across the entire theological spectrum are variously under way in terms short of single programs. Curriculum planning can move ahead without the uniformity of program; indeed, uniformity would not be desirable. *Two types of basic courses,* for example, may provide variety and experimentation in place of the six or ten which previously were given. Team teaching among faculties of diverse orientations frequently introduces new dimensions productive for students and professors alike. Electives can cover a wider scope and yet end the wasteful repetition of identical courses from different faculties, each with a few students, by the device of offering one course, and the same faculty person offering it twice if student demand warrants it. The latter is a fruitful device for teaching undergraduate and graduate sections, provided the problem of teaching loads is adequately met. Moreover, several schools can together inaugurate experimental programs, utilizing several students and a faculty member from each school.

The preceding suggests ways, some of which are already operative, for schools to work together in significant patterns, while maintaining their own integrity—a word to be distinguished from autonomy. Indeed, unless schools are willing to relinquish some autonomy because they believe there are specific goals for which it is worth giving up a few prerogatives, the efforts will not accomplish much and the added machinery will only be an irritant. Those of us who believe that the major integration of faculties at all levels is both desirable and inevitable also believe that patterns of cooperation in which the integrity of institutions is maintained can be set up so that further developments can take place without major readjustments. Cooperative structures of an institutional or semi-institutional nature can be created with enough flexibility to serve the whole. But such institutional arrangements will need to be flexible in order to respond to needed change, and leadership will require the role of being the servant of all.

## The Necessity of a New Type of Clergy

The critical issue is that institutions must now prepare a different type of clergy and laity in the light of three major developments: (1) the ecumenical reality; (2) an increasingly urban society; (3) a secular world no longer understood from a Christian point of view. Taken together, they dictate the end of the older conceptions of ministry and therefore demand new processes of ministerial formation.

Whatever the style which may be demanded for any group, we are now in an *ecumenical setting* in which we know enough about each other so that isolation from each other is no longer justifiable. We share many mutual theological concerns and so many historical judgments that we can no longer rightfully be allowed to be alone, but rather we can now accept the encounters with each other. We have a new responsibility, and those who resist it can hardly be argued against, but only resisted in turn—as many within both Catholicism and Protestantism are doing. The ecumenical fact is that we are wrong to be isolated from each other and had better get on with the common tasks that are demanded of us.

Working in an *urban area* demands a new educational style. Clergy of all traditions are now working in contact with each other in hospitals, chaplaincies, inner city, etc. Already their mission provides personal contact and, at appropriate junctures, also common actions and programs. Hence, theological education must take on the training of clergy in ways which make theological and personal contact across Church and other boundaries thoroughly natural. It must train for functional ministries through which differently oriented individuals work in harmony on programs and problems. Formation and training will have to take place in contexts and ways which already incorporate the style of work to be entered upon. Education and subsequent ministries are thus linked to each other, with the difference between them being that initially the educational aspects must be central, and later the correlative, sustaining and reforming aspects must be emphasized.

The third factor is the meaning for the ministry in that the *world is secular,* standing before us without assumed contexts of understanding. Certainly, everything is no longer Christian, or understood in a Christian way. But the older forms of ministry were formed precisely to function in a Christian world, or a world on the way to becoming Christian. Indeed, the ministry was trained and formed in life settings meant to be analogies to a Christian world. Formation thus was the determination of a form of life in which theological learning on its academic side was but one facet rather than the central facet. Perhaps this unrecognized motivation lay behind the founding of theological schools in the United States in isolation from urban centers and their distracting influences. It was felt that only such a circumscribed preparation could qualify priests and ministers for the conforming of the world to the ethos and ethic demanded of the Gospel. The ministry was a prototype and analogue of that style, though not the exhibition of the form of life directly to be imitated by everyone. Catholics recognized this distinction in what was expected of laity and clergy, and Protestants, while they thoroughly played down the distinction, equally manifested the laity-clergy division.

It is precisely this type of approach which is in question. The older idea of clergy as the instruments for the conforming of the world to the Gospel no longer is viable in a world which has become secular, in which the Gospel illumines existence and grace is appropriated in sacramental acts. Gone is the total explanation of all things. All things are no longer directly sacramentally understood. The Gospel now is more limited in the scope of what it covers, but more vibrant in what it teaches. A secular world at best is open for Christian participation. Clergy can no longer be the prototype of the Gospel in relation to the world, but the instrument, even the priestly instrument, of more limited focusings of the occasions and contexts of grace.

Precisely these changes demand a new conception of formation. Nothing less is involved in the movement of American theological schools to urban areas and to various levels of transconfessional integration. Given our world and what will be required in the light of the Gospel, a different clergy and a new formation are necessary. Things will not and dare not be the same. Unless change is courageously entered into for the sake of the Church, the Church herself will be the loser as the polarization increases between those who will hold on as the threat of change is greater and those who will become more strident as the resistance to change increases. The initial intoxication of new exposures and the vistas they open do lead some of the uninitiated either to throw over, or unduly bend, their heritage. Such reactions are usually short-lived. But they present major problems of patience for ecclesiastical officials who frequently, in their zeal for safeguarding the heritage, prematurely force a taking of alternatives. For most students, the experience is quite the contrary, for instead of a loss of tradition, they discover a heightening awareness of their own heritage—indeed, so much that it takes time for the full educational encounters to develop. The danger is not too much exposure, but far too little. Indeed, ecclesiastics could take comfort in theological faculties. They are more pervasively conservative than they are radical, and the new settings will demand more change than even they may be prepared to entertain. But caution may result in more mistakes due to restraint rather than those due to innovation.

If faculties continue to be isolated, the resultant formation will become irrelevant. There are signs that disaffection with the ministry is already the result of the isolation of faculties from each other and the world. Only an extensive relating of faculties, for which there is no single pattern, will provide a context for new experiments in the forming of clergy as well as the diverse and extensive resources demanded.

The conforming of the world to the Gospel, if we are dealing with the Christian context, cannot be thought of in single uniform patterns. It will occur at specific junctures or occasions. Therefore, no single type of formation or clergy will do. This demands the acceptance of many experiments, designed to create believers—clergy and laity alike—who are not cast into the same mold, for their ministries will be as multiple and variegated as the life settings themselves.

Such formation has more to do with life styles than with theological factors, though theology needs to be in harmony with formation. Perhaps theology may even form the style by its fruitful correlation of theology and life. Theological differences do divide much of Christendom, and Christendom and Judaism. But within Protestantism, theological differences are increasingly less important. Within Roman Catholicism, it is certainly not conceded that significant differences exist. What then is it that makes a Dominican a Dominican, and a Jesuit a Jesuit? Of course, there are different theological accents, and this raises the question for some of whether or not Dominicans and Jesuits ought to have the same teachers. But the accents are apparently related to an ethos, to a style of living and doing things. It is doubtful that the differences in formation rest in different understandings of Scripture, Church history, or even theology. They rest in the life experiences themselves.

The life style, while germane to one's heritage, must include the ecumenical and urban realities as both a training ground and the context for work. But the probable clue to formation in any heritage lies in the communities of life, including work and worship. There is a forming context, but its characteristics are life experiences associated with an ethos—discipline and rhythms of life, forms of worship and work, modes of leisure and recreation, ways of incorporating the surreptitious and the obvious impacts of the society around one. Theology is only, but significantly, the sea in which such currents are understood and sometimes redirected.

If such orientations are taken seriously, the clergy will no longer be the prototype of the older conforming of the world to Christ. While more functional and set apart also by sacramental functionings, they will be believers whose affinity to the issues of life will make all priests and all believers without abolishing the distinctions. They will be formed as the spiritual ambassadors and facilitators of the occasions of grace which redirect the world about them with its endless, tantalizing possibilities.

### The Future

Concrete results of such developing educational processes can only be mentioned. There can surely be little doubt that the ecumenical educational venture will overcome many divisions now centuries old. New fields of academic work will emerge, not new in the sense of being added—for that has happened all too often—but new in the reshaping or replacing of older disciplines in the light of new cooperative work. University resources will be utilized more extensively, with less reliance exclusively on the arts and sciences faculties. New fruitful relations will develop with university professional schools and with institutes devoted to special problems. Cooperative library programs, based on emerging scientific advances, will make new centers of research and learning available in areas where resources can be combined and extended. Faculty planning across schools will make it possible to fill gaps and enter into new areas. Judaism and the history of religions will no longer be grist for the Christian mill, but will enter fully into the dialogical possibilities of our time.

John Bennett/*New York, New York*

# Ecumenical Cooperation on Public Issues

T here is a remarkable convergence between Roman Catholic teaching and policy on the major problems of society and the thought that has been developing within the ecumenical movement that is associated with the World Council of Churches. Most of the obstacles to mutual understanding and cooperation on these issues have been removed. For example, the fear of Roman Catholic power, especially in relation to the religious freedom of non-Catholics, has largely disappeared. This is in part the effect of the *Declaration on Religious Freedom* of Vatican Council II, but it also comes out of the experience that Protestants have had of the spirit of openness and freedom among Roman Catholics since the Council. There have been innumerable contacts on all levels between Protestants and Catholics which have created a mutual confidence that was rare ten years ago.

One illustration of this change can be seen in the difference in the attitude of American Protestants toward the idea of a Roman Catholic president in 1960 as compared with the outlook today. The year 1960 was marked by a great deal of ugly anti-Catholicism because of the candidacy of John F. Kennedy. In the past year the Roman Catholicism of both the late Senator Robert F. Kennedy and Senator Eugene McCarthy was hardly noticed.

The fear of a monolithic Roman Catholicism directed from one center has ceased to be a significant political factor in the United States where it had been very strong.

The encyclical of Pope Paul on birth control called attention to the one remaining major difference on social policy between Catholics and Protestants, but even this most unfortunate event made clear that there is no Catholic monolith and revealed that many Catholic theologians and laymen had gained freedom to express their opposition to papal teaching on this subject. If this were not the case, cooperation between Protestants and Catholics on many social issues would continue, but for a time the present spontaneous mutual confidence would be threatened. Even as it is there will be times of difficulty when official bodies work together on "development" in the "third world" for which the papal teaching on birth control creates so great an obstacle.

## Social Teaching

Several decades before the Council it was evident that there was a basic convergence between Catholic and Protestant thinking on the issues of social justice and on the role of free enterprise and its relation to the responsibility of the State. What Max Weber called the "Protestant ethic" (the ethic of late Puritanism rather than of the Reformers), which did have an important part in the encouraging of modern economic individualism, still remains as a cultural force in some countries, but the teaching of Protestant Church councils and of most Protestant theologians with ecumenical influence has been highly critical of the institutions of capitalism. This came to a head on a world scale at the Amsterdam Assembly of the World Council of Churches in 1948 where the ideology of *laissez faire* capitalism was attacked explicitly. This criticism of capitalism for long had been supported by the teaching of such influential theologians as Archbishop William Temple, Karl Barth, Reinhold Niebuhr and Paul Tillich. All four of these thinkers represented some form of "Christian Socialism" which verbally at least was opposed by papal teaching.

The emphasis on Christian Socialism lost influence after World War II but I think that its permanent effect was the overcoming of the individualism of the "Protestant ethic". In the United States the whole movement known as the Social Gospel had this same effect.

The basis for the convergence to which I refer may be seen in the fact that Protestant thinking moved away from the ethic of economic individualism, while Catholic teaching had never embraced it. Protestants with ecumenical influence did not take the negative attitude toward socialism that characterized Roman Catholic teaching. They even were often open to the contributions of Marxism and were hopeful about the possibilities of co-operation with Communist societies. Pope John XXIII came to express this hope, and the initiation by Roman Catholics of dialogue with Marxists has reduced one element of tension between Protestants and Catholics. In some countries, not least in the United States, the absolutistic anti-Communism of Roman Catholic authorities was a point of real difficulty, but today Roman Catholics often take the lead in the dialogue with Marxists.

The convergence between ecumenical Protestant and Roman Catholic social teaching has transcended these ideological conflicts. Both Protestant teaching (and here I include the teaching of the World Council of Churches which includes Eastern Orthodox) and Roman Catholic teaching as expressed in encyclicals and in the *Constitution on the Church in the Modern World* of Vatican Council II seek a mixed society which recognizes the need of private property and individual initiative and, in various forms, the principle of "subsidiarity", and both make room for increasing the initiative of the State in economic life. The concept of "the responsible society" which was first set forth at the Amsterdam Assembly has been a continuing element in the teaching of the World Council of Churches, and I think that it is almost identical with the main tendency in *Mater et Magistra, Pacem in Terris* and *Populorum Progresssio* in regard to the relations between the State and the participation of individuals and of various intermediate groups. The following quotation from the report of the Third Section of the Evanston Assembly of the World Council of Churches (1954) illustrates this:

> While the State is sometimes the enemy of freedom, under many circumstances the State is the only instrument that can make freedom possible for large sectors of the population. The State is not the source of social justice, but it must be its guardian, ready if necessary to accept responsibility to counteract depression or inflation and to relieve the impact of unemployment, industrial injury, low wages, and unfavorable working conditions, sickness and old age. But in doing so the State remains the servant and not the lord of social justice. Therefore we must warn against the danger that the union of political and economic power may result in an all-controlling State.

This passage even has the characteristic of papal documents, for it combines balance and ambiguity to leave room for many experiments in different situations. But as a basis for overcoming the deposits of the individualistic "Protestant ethic" or of an uncritical statism, this statement gives real guidance to the Churches.

## Development and Revolution

In the past two years especially there has been convergence to a marked degree on the responsibility of Churches and Christians to apply these principles of social justice to the relations between rich and poor nations, to the problems of "development." The report of the Geneva Conference on Church and Society which was convened by the World Council of Churches in 1966 and the encyclical *Populorum Progressio* are remarkably similar in outlook. The fourth Assembly of the World Council of Churches at Uppsala in 1968 gave massive support on a more official level to the work of the Geneva Conference in this area. Meanwhile the collaboration between the World Council and the papal Commission on Justice and Peace has underlined the importance of the convergence to which I refer. Except for the one question of birth control which is indeed very fateful for issues of development, there is remarkable harmony between Protestant and World Council thinking and official Roman Catholic thinking.

When we speak of "development" we immediately have the question thrust upon us of the relation between development and revolution. At the Geneva Conference, for the first time the Churches of Asia, Africa and Latin America were strongly represented in ecumenical discussions of the affairs of their continents. It came to be realized that the thinking of the World Council had been too much oriented toward nations with long established legal traditions, toward Western countries that had already achieved a measure of stability in relating the claims of social justice to the institutions of order. The rise of "black power" at the heart of the life of the United States with strong revolutionary demands indicates that even to say that these problems are on their way to solution in the West is an overstatement. Though revolution need not involve violence, if it is a planned displacement of those who now have political or economic power, it is likely to be accompanied by violence.

Consideration of this whole range of problems involving the universal viability of established Western political and legal institutions and involving the initiation of illegal actions and violence as a last resort for the sake of justice is only on the fringe of official Protestant and Catholic teaching. In this area we all face the same theoretical and practical problems. Official Roman Catholic documents and World Council documents refer to the problem of revolutionary violence in much the same way. They note all of the risks and ambiguities that accompany violence or any breakdown of the legal systems of order. *Populorum Progressio* by implication makes room for violent or illegal revolutionary activities "where there is a manifest, long-standing tyranny which would do great damage to fundamental personal rights and dangerous harm to the common good of the country" (n. 31). The World Council statements in several places give clearer permission for revolutionary violence as a last resort. At the Geneva Conference there was a tendency in speeches, though not in formal reports, to take a romantic attitude toward revolution. The delegates from Latin America were the chief exponents of revolution. Father Camilo Torres, the priest who joined the guerrillas in Colombia, was often referred to as a hero-martyr. At Uppsala much less was heard about revolution.

One of the most balanced statements of this issue was made by a group of theologians from many countries, including a strong delegation of Roman Catholics, at Zagorsk, a suburb of Moscow, in March 1968. While this statement warns against the illusions and the ambiguities involved in movements of revolutionary violence, it says the following: "But we must realize that some Christians find themselves where they must, in all responsibility, participate fully in the revolution with all of its inevitable violence." (This report is published in the World Council of Churches journal *Study Encounter*, Vol. IV, No. 2, 1968.) There must be much more thinking about the criteria for a just revolution to parallel what has long been done in the context of the "just war".

*War and Peace*

Another area in which there is a very strong common basis for thinking and action is that of war and peace. Already there is much in common in what the World Council and Protestant denominations and theologians say about nuclear war or the current threat of total war. Absolute pacifism, marginal in terms of the number of its adherents, has had considerable influence on Protestant thinking, but it has never had influence on official Roman Catholic teaching. There is among both Protestants and Catholics an area of convergence where both come ever closer to the complete rejection of war that involves the destruction of centers of population. Vatican Council II (*Constitution on the Church in the Modern World*, n. 80), in strongly rejecting such forms of warfare, avoids a specific reference to nuclear weapons. The Uppsala Assembly, following the report of the Geneva Conference, spoke of nuclear weapons and nuclear war. It said: "The Churches must insist that it is the first duty of governments to prevent such a war, to halt the present arms race, and to agree never to initiate the use of nuclear weapons." There are interim problems of deterrence, there is no agreement about what should be said about the *possession* in contrast to the *use* of nuclear weapons, and the principle of "double effect" easily becomes an excuse for evading the moral teaching about the use of such weapons, but we can expect the Churches to surround nuclear war and policies that are likely to lead to nuclear war with ever stronger religious and moral restraints. A single, all-encompassing absolute may still elude us, but that should not prevent Christians from seeking now to keep preparation for nuclear war and political steps that may lead to it under overwhelming moral criticism. Both Catholics and Protestants have moved away from the temptation to see any war against Communism as justified, as a "holy war", and the disappearance of the idea of an "absolute enemy" should remove all excuse to contemplate the use of the "absolute weapon."

The cooperation between Catholics and Protestants should extend to the prevention of ideological and counter-revolutionary wars of intervention. There has been a noticeable difference between the pope's attitude toward the war in Vietnam and that of the American hierarchy. The war in Vietnam has revealed for all to see some of the limits of military power in bringing about social solutions. (It is to be hoped that the Soviet Union will soon learn about these limits in connection with its brutal and stupid intervention in Czechoslovakia.) I foresee that in the next decade the great involvement of the Roman Catholic Church in Latin America may create major problems of thought and policy both in regard to revolutions and in regard to military interventions by outside powers. The influence of the Catholic Church in the United States in regard to American policy to Latin America remains uncertain. My impression is that worldwide Catholicism and worldwide Protestantism will bring pressure upon both Catholics and Protestants in the United States to use their influence against a policy of military intervention to prevent revolution in Latin America. Christian thought must be focused on this problem. The resolution of the Uppsala Assembly on Vietnam put major emphasis on the war in Vietnam as an example of what not to do in the future. Among other things it said: "The appalling situation of the Vietnamese people today offers an example of the tragedy to which unilateral intervention of a great power can lead." The problem will be to find a path that avoids both this kind of interventionism and isolationism on the part of great powers.

*Special Difficulties*

I shall now deal with two issues that accompany all cooperative thought and action about the particular problems that I have mentioned and others similar to them: (1) the way in which the common morality associated in Roman Catholic thought with natural law is understood; (2) the fact that no Church, Catholic or Protestant, is fully agreed about these problems.

The present cooperation between Catholics and Protestants has been helped by the great restraint in Catholic circles in the use of the concept of *natural law*. Natural law is one of the chief subjects of debate between Catholic teaching and much Protestant teaching. However, many Catholics are rethinking their interpretation of natural law, and Protestants, whatever their theory, do take for granted a common ground morality that, while not necessarily universally recognized, does make possible cooperation on matters of justice and peace between Christians and non-Christians; such facts represent another area of convergence. One reason that the pope's encyclical on birth control was such a shock was that it was a case of retrogression to a view of natural law now widely abandoned in Roman Catholic circles and clearly not a deliverance of human reason but rather of a narrow and ecclesiastically preserved tradition.

In attempting to spell out the broadly based morality which

Catholics and Protestants take for granted in spite of debates about natural law, there has been a common use of the category of "the human". This does not enable us to rationally deduce many specific laws which are absolute in themselves, but it does help to define the main criteria for society, the main conditions that must be met if mankind is to achieve a truly human existence. The report of the Geneva Conference in its discussion of the problems of development and *Populorum Progressio* both stress the human as the norm. Obviously while this provides a basis for a common understanding of some of the ends of society, it calls for a new agenda of cooperative thinking about what constitutes the human. We are more sure about some things that are inhuman than we are about the political and social and cultural patterns which in positive terms and in a time of rapid change are most favorable to a fully human life. Both Catholics and Protestants can recognize that there is a common program here and also that there are many elements in the program that remain open.

The second problem is raised by the fact that there remains so much *disagreement within the Churches* even about matters which on the ecumenical level seem most assured. Protestants can expect this to be the case. There is no authority which can do more than commend to them, with some weight, convictions which they may or may not accept as true. I doubt if there is much difference here between Catholics and Protestants in spite of the differences of ecclesiastical structure. There are divisions in both religious communities that come from nationalism and provincialism and the pressures of immediate economic interest, and there are divisions that arise out of the differences between conservative and progressive habits of mind. Catholics and Protestants face the same opposition at the grass roots on issues of racial justice to the very clear teaching of the Churches. In the United States there has been an interesting difference between the national leadership of the Protestant Churches and that of the Roman Catholic hierarchy on Vietnam. The former has been more critical of the war policy of the government than the latter.

Protestant leaders have often appealed to Roman Catholic bishops, asking them to follow the leadership of the pope on Vietnam. There has been strong resistance on the part of conservative lay Protestant leadership in local Churches to the national leaders of denominations and of the National and World Councils of Churches on this issue, just as there has been very forceful opposition to most of the Catholic hierarchy on the part of progressive groups of Catholic clergy and laymen on the same issue. I use this example to illustrate the contention that Catholics and Protestants face a similar problem.

There is no final formal solution of this problem. If there were, the Roman Catholics would have found it. Many of them know as well as Protestants that authority depends upon response, that no magisterial fiat can take the place of the authority of that which has intrinsic truth. Such encyclicals as *Pacem in Terris* and *Populorum Progressio* have more authority to convince both Catholics and Protestants than the encyclical on birth control.

I believe that we should deal with this problem of authority in two ways. The first is through processes that enable councils of the Church on many levels to speak and teach and act on the basis of careful preparation. Even a democratic Church cannot expect to receive Christian guidance by means of a Gallup Poll of the members. Those who can speak and teach need to have gone through the kind of education that enables them to see what the distinctive meaning of the Christian message is for social problems and that corrects views which result from national and provincial pressures and the pressures of economic interest to which I have referred. Clergy (including bishops) and laymen need this kind of experience. Vatican Council II and the assemblies and conferences of the World Council of Churches have had this corrective influence.

Also, there should be emphasis on unofficial, voluntary movements that are devoted to the particular problems of justice and peace. The creativity of the official Church can be seen in its encouraging of these movements to develop within its life. Official bodies are cautious; they often prefer silence, or the repetition of old formulae that now fail to convince. The stirring of the air and the debate on issues which the Church needs for its own illumination can often come best from these nonofficial movements. Student movements, lay journals, organized groups of theologians or lay experts, faculties that have academic freedom and unions of Christians who have common concerns or commitments in regard to the more controversial social issues provide much of the vitality and the new thinking that stimulate the official Church to face the problems that it may seek to evade. They prod it to think, to speak and to act. When movements of this kind are interconfessional, they help to prepare the way for official interconfessional cooperation on many levels.

Jan Witte, S.J./*Rome, Italy*

# From Theological Discussion to Concrete Results in Ecumenism

We have now had sixty years of an ecumenical movement, twenty years of a World Council of Churches, and ten years of a Secretariate for Unity, and many people ask impatiently whether all this theological discussion could not have produced some more concrete results. Should the Churches not have come closer together in doctrine and practice? Sometimes this impatience turns to a kind of ecumenical activism which thinks it can well do without all those theological profundities. On the side of the theologians there is not infrequently a certain lassitude, perhaps because these discussions seem to float in a too purely intellectual atmosphere without anybody being compelled to take any concrete steps; perhaps this also results because of the official doctrinal position of various Churches with regard to controversial issues, a position which, in view of the constant change in the "front lines" where the ecumenical theologians are placed, seems to lie in a hinterland so hopelessly far behind the actuality that they wonder whether all contact is lost.

This impatience and this lassitude make our problem an urgent one. In this demand for "concrete ecumenical results", one might think of solutions for *practical* problems, either in the context of concrete worldwide problems, or, in the context of inter-Church relations, of solutions for such problems as the mutual

recognition of each other's baptism, mixed marriages or intercommunion. Confrontation with the actual existence of several
Churches outside one's own and openness toward the needs of
the whole world, for the salvation of which Christ founded his
Church, give "ecclesial" theology truly new dimensions which no
"theological discussion" can ignore.

But one can also look at "concrete ecumenical results" in
another way. One can think of theological discussion as concerned with the deeply rooted attitudes which have kept us separated in doctrine and practice for so many centuries. One may
wonder what conditions must be fulfilled to bring about concrete
results at this level, and how such a theological discussion can
already bring us Christians and our Churches together to a
greater unity and a purer, fuller understanding of the Gospel.
This seems to us to be the key issue which we were asked to deal
with, as well as the key issue for the solution of the *practical*
ecumenical problems just mentioned.

## The Basis for the "Theological Discussion"

The point of such a discussion lies in an actual encounter
between Christians of different doctrine and religious practice,
and this encounter must have an existential character because
the discussion concerns the very roots of these differences. Such
an encounter can only be meaningful and bear fruit if the partners in the dialogue are firmly rooted in their own convictions.
The "conversation" does not run on the lines of the highly individual opinions of Mr. A and Mr. B, but aims at testing the basic
convictions of their Churches with their respective doctrine and
practice by their evangelical value. In traditional terms, one may
simply say that the partners must be theologians who are truly
representative of their Churches. This holds, of course, for all
theologians, and there are numerous levels at which such ecumenically pointed theological discussions can occur: chance encounters between individual persons, or small, unofficial discussion groups, right up to the meetings of the official theological
commissions appointed by the separated Churches, even though

this "official" character can in no sense bind the Churches represented.

Since it is at this last level that the conditions for concrete ecumenical results and the manner in which they can be achieved may be most clearly observed, I limit myself from now on to these "official conversations", without in any way wanting to underrate the importance of the many other levels of discussion. For the meaning of "ecclesial theology" I refer to Karl Rahner who dealt with it in a recent article about the ecclesial dialogue within the Church—not the inter-Church dialogue—entitled "The New Ecclesial Character of Theology".[1] We may briefly summarize his view of the conditions for a dialogue between the Church's magisterium and the theologians as follows: the magisterium must respect the theologian's freedom of conscience without authoritarian indoctrination, but also without leaving them entirely to an unadulterated individualism that operates outside the context of a Church animated by the Spirit; in particular, it must recognize the creative and critical function of the theologian. On his part, the theologian "must recognize as binding upon himself such teaching of the Church as she maintains and teaches with absolute commitment and which she cannot separate from her faith and her self-understanding." [2]

I fully agree with this, and therefore thought that this *formal* aspect of "ecclesiality" should be mentioned in this article about ecumenical "theological discussion". Unfortunately, and no doubt because of necessary limitations, Rahner mentions only this purely formal aspect, so that we hear practically nothing about the problem of the *content* which this ecclesiality envisages. As a result, practically nothing is really said about the "new" ecclesial character of theology: "Perhaps I have only spoken of the old ecclesial character. But this seems to me, even in the sober and often sad ordinariness of ecclesial theology, quite definitely always new." [3] Agreed, but Rahner's article

[1] K. Rahner, "Die neue Kirchlichkeit der Theologie. Statt eines Selbstporträts," in *Geist und Leben* 41 (1968), pp. 205-16.

[2] Cf., for the first part, *ibid.*, p. 216; for the second part, *ibid.*, p. 213.

[3] *Ibid.*, p. 215: "I should have spoken of the new ecclesiality of theol-

might make us overlook that, if the formal ecclesial aspect remains the same, or must remain the same, the content at which this ecclesial loyalty aims is subject to changes, and has in fact so developed during the last decades that we have to talk about a "new" ecclesiality, and that we must see what this newness consists of. This newness becomes prominent in the "theological conversation". Does the ecclesial loyalty of the theologians who take part in it demand that they stubbornly cling to solutions of theological problems as defined in history? Is this ecclesial loyalty the same as being stubborn—*semper idem* (always the same)?

Many have held this view of loyalty for a long time, particularly in the Roman Catholic Church. The correct ecclesial loyalty was then exclusively directed, insofar as the content was concerned, to one's own Church, with its own confession and other pronouncements. Forms of Christian communities outside one's own Church were not entitled to the name of "Church", at least not "dogmatically", so it was said. Here the Roman Catholic Church was the most radical, although in practice at least this exclusivism was not unknown in other Churches, too. Such exclusive views, or at least attitudes, about one's own Church only permitted "converting the other", and a theological discussion on equal footing was impossible.

Such "equal footing" does not have to imply a leveling down of all Churches, but it *does* demand the recognition of some ecclesiality in other Christian communities as such, and therefore the recognition of a Christian doctrine and practice peculiar to such communities. The *newness* in ecclesiality arises particularly when a Church becomes aware that there is room in its own understanding of "Church" for the admission of peculiar ecclesial elements in the other Christian communities, something that is their own but is Christian in doctrine and practice. This does not make one less "loyal" than before; it does not imply that one

---

ogy, but perhaps I have only spoken of the old one. But this appears to me always as new even in the sober and often sad ordinariness of ecclesial theology."

puts one's own individual smugness, one's own individual opinion, above the judgment of the Church, but that one goes back, with all loyalty to the definitively declared content and purpose of the confession, to the ultimate foundation of all ecclesial loyalty, which is faithfulness to Christ and his Word. We seek to confront the partly historically conditioned form of confession and the spiritual climate of our own age with our broadened concept of the Church and with the Word of Christ. We then draw the conclusions for our contemporary way of proclaiming this Word and also for our new formulation of ecclesial teaching. Where the old ecclesial loyalty knows how to work with this new broadening of concepts, we discover the common basis for genuine ecumenical theological discussion.

For Roman Catholic theology, this space-to-move-in was really only discovered at Vatican Council II, where an awareness emerged that "ecclesiality" was not simply identical with the ecclesiality of the Roman Catholic Church. After the *Constitution on the Church* had described the mystery of the Church of Christ in its first chapter, an attempt was made to state clearly that the invisible and the visible Church are one. Article 8 leaves no doubt that the Church described as mystery is not an invisible "Church of love", separated from the juridically organized Church. There is a concrete unity of one-in-two, where the visible reality is precisely the "sign" of the presence of the Spirit who operates *in* and *through* the Church, and so this Church is the sacrament of unity in Christ through the Spirit. In order to emphasize this a draft of 1963 read: *"Therefore* this Church (i.e., this one, holy, catholic and apostolic Church, founded by Christ), the true mother and teacher of all men, instituted in this world and organized as a society, *is* the Catholic Church which is governed by the pope and the bishops united with him." [4] One can sense the strict identification. But the protests of a number of the Council fathers caused this formula to be changed in the final draft: "This Church, constituted and organized in the world as a

[4] Cf. *Lexicon f. Theol. u. Kirche, Das II Vat. Konzil I,* p. 174, n. 29 where there is a reference to Mühlen I, note 26).

society, subsists in the Catholic Church, which is governed by the successor of Peter and by the bishops in union with that successor, although many elements of sanctification and of truth can be found outside of her visible structure. These elements, however, as gifts properly belonging to the Church of Christ, possess an inner dynamisn toward Catholic unity." [5] The strict identification has clearly fallen out; "therefore" has been dropped and "is" has been replaced by "subsists in", [6] while ecclesial elements outside the Roman Catholic Church are frankly recognized.

Although this text does not say everything that could be said, it is clear that here a crowbar was applied to ecclesial exclusiveness. Room has been made for other Christian communities. "Ecclesiality" is henceforth no longer identical with what belongs exclusively to the Roman Catholic Church. It is clear that these ecclesial elements outside the Roman Catholic Church, which are "gifts properly belonging to the Church of Christ", do not exclude the specific character of the separated "Churches". Grateful use of this crowbar was made in the *Decree on Ecumenism* when the "ecclesial" character of the other "Churches" and "ecclesial communities" was debated. [7] The second chapter of the *Constitution on the Church* about the People of God also contributed significantly to the broadening of the ideas of "Church" and "ecclesiality" because it put the catholicity of the Church in a new light: the Church exists for the sake of the world, and here she is the unique sign of salvation in Christ.

And with this "uniqueness" of the sign of salvation we have landed ourselves in the scandalous—because sinful—anomaly of the unique Church of Christ and all the analogous Churches which cannot be ignored, from our point of view. This scandal of unity in division is one of which not a single Church is innocent. Faced with this fact, we cannot rest content with that "union-

[5] Based on a Dutch translation by G. Philips in *Constit. en Decreten van het tweede Vat. Oec. Concilie* V, p. 23.

[6] Cf. *Lex. f. Theol. u. Kirche,* op. cit., p. 173.

[7] Cf. *Decree on Ecumenism*, nn. 14-24, about the Word of revelation, the sacraments and the office as being *also proper* to the other "Churches" and "ecclesial communities".

ism", that demand for a return to the Catholic Church with a minimum of self-criticism and concessions. With all the enduring awareness of our Church's foundation by Christ himself, the Roman Catholic Church should now seriously reflect on her historical character and on the sins and narrow-mindedness which have hampered her obedience to her calling in spite of all the divinely warranted, fundamental loyalty to Christ, so that the joyful message can be proclaimed to the whole world in the unity of all Christians, as happened at Vatican Council II.

I have briefly sketched the growth toward a new ecclesiality in the Roman Catholic Church. But the other Churches were struggling with a similar problem. On many points Vatican Council II gave them a helpful example. The surprising result of the last decade has been that, insofar as we know from our own experience and published or unpublished reports, a new "ecclesiality" has emerged practically everywhere in the official ecumenical "theological conversations". This in no way implies a denial of loyalty to one's own Church but rather an inclusion of the other Churches in one way or another according to content of the ultimate aim. This vague indication is now growing into a richly varied pattern as we try to see how, on the basis of this "new ecclesiality", concrete ecumenical results *can* be reached and in fact *have been* achieved.

## Achieving Concrete Ecumenical Results

There is no point in idealizing the situation. Obviously, not all the participants in the official discussions understand or accept the new ecclesiality in the sense I have indicated. Some may also be lacking in loyalty to their own Church. But I think that we can substantiate with many facts (sometimes merely referred to, for brevity's sake) the point that the general direction of this kind of theological discussion has been excellent during the last ten years. For this we have studied the reports of some official conversations between the World Council and Roman Catholics, between the Lutheran World Federation (referred to as L.W.F.) and Roman Catholics, between the Lutheran Churches of the

United States and Roman Catholics, between the American Episcopalians and Roman Catholics, between the L.W.F. and the World Council of Calvinist Churches ("The World Alliance of Reformed Churches" = W.A.R.C.). This is already a far-reaching list, but it is far from complete. I am not competent to speak of the discussions between Eastern Orthodox and Roman Catholic theologians, and have only superficial knowledge of the discussions between Anglicans and Methodists in England.

What strikes one in all these discussions is the courage and openness with which the problems are tackled from scratch. For once they did not start from each one's own tradition and a consequent sharp opposition, but rather by reading the scriptures afresh and without prejudice. This does not mean, of course, that they abandoned their own tradition beforehand, and certainly not their own dogma. But it *did* mean that they asked what really was essential in all these texts taken together, without emphasis placed on the material used for traditional "proofs" for one's own opinion. Here the first step was obviously taken by the exegetes so that the literal meaning could be established, and this was then followed by the proper ecumenical work, which included penetrating into the thought of non-Roman Catholics. As a result, the Reformers as well as modern Protestant and Orthodox authors, Fathers of the Church, St. Thomas, papal and conciliar declarations and authors such as Rahner, Ratzinger, Schillebeeckx, Congar and Küng, have all been referred to. This is a laborious task where one has to try to express oneself without prejudice in the language and mentality of the other in order to avoid misunderstanding and yet in such a way that there is no contortion of one's own doctrine. One has to take into account the historical and emotional elements which play along with certain expressions. One has to ask: What does this reply of the other to this theological question really mean in his mind? And what do we really mean when we give the answer of our own Church? Would the now agreed interpretation of Scripture give us a new starting point to find an agreed answer to a problem that is loaded with historical ballast?

When we turn to the reports, we are struck by the fact that all follow a more or less similar procedure, as described above (I shall soon take up an important qualification on this point). And what are the results? Let us look at some examples.

At the Amsterdam Assembly of the World Council of Churches in 1948, the "catholicity" of the Church was discussed, but there "Catholic plenitude" was sharply contrasted with "evangelical purity", and this led to a division of the Churches into those of a "Catholic" and those of a "Protestant" type, which led Karl Barth to warn them against yielding to "confessional cramp." Now, Uppsala has shown convincingly that it is not only possible but already a fact that this "confessional cramp" can be overcome without disloyalty to one's own deepest religious convictions. The new ecclesiality managed to strip the notion of "catholicity" of its connotation of "that which belongs exclusively to the Roman Catholic Church". The awareness that the one Church of Christ does not exclusively "subsist" in the Roman Catholic Church implied that the catholicity of that Church, too, was not her exclusive property but belongs also, at least analogously, to the other Christian Churches. On the Protestant side it came to be admitted that "evangelical purity", too, is no longer seen as the exclusive property of the Protestant Churches, which have also become increasingly aware of a lack of "Catholic plenitude" in their own tradition.

In the meantime a mixed commission of the World Council and the Roman Catholic Church was busy with the problem of "the Church's catholicity and apostolicity". Here again we were struck by the concentration on christology in the matter of ecclesiology. It was soon agreed that the "catholicity" of the Church is rooted in and everlastingly borne by the presence of the risen Christ through the Holy Spirit wherever believers are gathered together in his name, where his Word is proclaimed, where his sacraments are administered and particularly where the eucharist is celebrated. This new approach, in which Catholics started from sacramentality and Protestants from eschatology, surprisingly revealed a methodological parallelism which led to the common conviction that it is precisely through the presence of the risen Christ that the Church is in this world the present *sacramental sign* of the final *eschatological fulfillment* (which is in fact nothing but the full and perfect presence of the risen Lord to all those who are saved). No doubt, this does not yet give us immediate *practical* results, but who would deny that a concrete ecumenical result has been achieved in the mutual understanding and appreciation in sacramental doctrine and eschatology, and in this growing toward a common interpretation of catholicity and apostolicity (understood not only through the past but also from the present situation and the eschatological orientation)? Moreover, the consequences of this for the teaching on baptism and the eucharist are obvious. And in order to see how we are growing together in the teaching on baptism and the eucharist, it is particularly instructive to look at the other "official theological conversation" between American Lutheran and Roman Catholic theologians, who have already published three booklets on their discussion in a handy format and at a very low price.[8]

Here they found, so it seems to us, the right way of making their work known to members of their own Churches and interested members of the public. For the commission has not only a responsible task to fulfill *during* the discussion, but also afterward so that their progress and failures and final achievements can really penetrate into the Church or Churches within their terms of reference. Unfortunately, these terms are sometimes too narrowly conceived so that the result does not get known beyond the office of a high ecclesiastical authority. But in this way the trite prejudices about another Church's doctrine and practice cannot be overcome in the members of one's own faith, and thus the "concrete ecumenical results" will hardly be turned into

[8] Cf. the Representatives of the U.S.A. National Committee of the Lutheran World Federation and the Bishops' Commission for Ecumenical Affairs: I. *The Status of the Nicene Creed as Dogma of the Church* (Nat. Cath. Welfare Conf., 1965); II. *One Baptism for the Remission of Sins* (*ibid.*, 1966); III. *The Eucharist as Sacrifice* (*ibid.*, 1968), all three obtainable from Publications Office, U.S. Cath. Conf., 1312 Massachusetts Avenue, N.W., Washington D.C. 20005.

practical decisions. Many a discussion on practical issues has been protracted over the years, and it is here that it needs the injection of a new broad vision, based on a fresh understanding of Christ's Word and seen in the light of this age. We recommend particularly the second and third of these booklets. The second, entitled *One Baptism for the Remission of Sins* not only clears up a whole series of misunderstandings in a few competent essays from both sides, but also leads to the conclusion that there is "substantial agreement" on the doctrine of baptism between the Lutheran Churches in the U. S. A. and the Roman Catholic Church.

The agreement is hardly less in the doctrine on the eucharist, at least on the two main points examined in *The Eucharist as Sacrifice*—namely, the eucharist as sacrifice and the presence of Christ in this sacrament. There appears to be no essential difference about the eucharist as a sacrifice of praise, gratitude and intercession. But what about the sacrifice of reconciliation (*propitiatorium*)? The commission states that "Catholics interpret this position today as a powerful emphasis on the fact that the presence of the one-and-only reconciling sacrifice of the cross in the Church's eucharistic celebration is effective for the forgiveness of sins and the life of the world. Up to this point Lutherans agree with them." [9] But, in spite of the still serious difficulties that remain, this is already great progress, particularly in connection with the office, a point with which the commission did not deal.

Thus, the *manner* and *duration* of Christ's presence in the eucharist is still a debated issue, but the main points of the "real", "true" and even "substantial" presence of Christ under the signs of bread and wine are already fully agreed upon. Are these not important, concrete ecumenical results? And how were they achieved? Again, by the same method: a willing listening to Scripture as the starting point (it is indeed a matter of Christ, the Lord of the Church, and his Word), then the clarification of the traditional formulas of both sides in the light of the 20th century, and, finally, the fearless, yet cautious and loyal interpretation of

[9] Cf. *The Eucharist as Sacrifice*, p. 190.

each other's point of view. History repeats itself in the discussions between American Episcopalians and Roman Catholics—the same method, the same surprising results—and then once again in the very successful discussions between the L.W.F. and the W.A.R.C., where it proved simply impossible to maintain any reason for a continued division between the Lutheran and the Calvinist Churches. Here, too, it was the "new ecclesiality" with its Lutheran and Calvinist nuances which produced a rich ecumenical harvest.

I have given a sketch of this "new ecclesiality", but there is one aspect which must be more strongly emphasized because it occurs in every "conversation" and often has a decisive influence, and that is the broadness of time and space which opens up whenever one looks behind any of the problems. There is always a concern with the world, for which the Church was founded, and with the *eschaton* toward which both Church and world are moving. It is not a matter of vague distances. The point is how Scripture and tradition can help us now to find that particular answer for the needs and problems of that mankind which surrounds us so that it will bring all closer to the *eschaton,* to the "new mankind", to Christ's nearness to us. That is why as theologians we no longer look exclusively toward our own Church—her glory, her pronouncements (however unconditionally we accept her dogma), her image, worship and spirituality—but at the same time to the other Churches, as well as the evolutions and revolutions of this world with its doubts, fears and needs. It is there that in the ecumenical theological discussion we meet the others no longer as "others" but as Christians with a common vocation for that world in need.

# PART II
## BIBLIOGRAPHICAL
## SURVEY

# How Can Ecumenical Understanding Be Furthered by the Theologian?

A Catholic Viewpoint
Maurice Villain, S.M., Paris, France

There was a time when the theologian who wanted to voice a non-traditional truth risked his career, if not his life. Boldness and courage were hardly to be recommended. Those days are gone forever, we hope. But boldness and courage in theology are not to be confused with presumptuous rashness and foolhardy impudence.

The theologian must always remain faithful to revelation in his work, especially today when the crisis confronting the faith raises questions about ecumenism rather than bolstering it. If the theologian clearly sees that his ideas are well founded, then he certainly must advance them with courage, but he will always do this humbly, maintaining contact with the living source through prayer and contemplation. How else could his thrust be prophetic?

Abbé Paul Couturier adopted an attitude of "prudent boldness"; as a result, this humble priest had an impact on the whole Church and effected a Copernican revolution in ecumenism. He changed the *insular* prayer of Catholics for the conversion of their separated brethren into *wide-open* prayer by all Christians "for the unity Christ wills for his Church."

Within the vast horizon of ecumenical theology, this article must focus on certain points that relate to the main problems confronting us. Our choice will be governed by our present-day situation, and by the needs and critical issues which surfaced at the recent meeting of the World Council of Churches in Uppsala.[1] In short, we shall focus on several problems of a doctrinal nature, leaving aside the question of joint ecumenical activity, for that seems to be the thrust of the question we have been asked.

Now it seems to me that the Catholic theologian can offer his services in three directions: (1) exploring the mystery of God with his Protestant brothers; (2) examining problems tied up with eucharistic communion; (3) molding public opinion and, by prayer, laying the groundwork for the entry of the Roman Catholic Church into the World Council of Churches.

## Exploring the Mystery of God

To put it bluntly, this may be the most urgent, if not the boldest, task for promoting ecumenical understanding. In the year 1967-1968, a "Year of Faith" for Catholics, their Church and all the Christian Churches have been shaken by a pervasive crisis of faith. Dr. E. C. Blake, the Secretary General of the WCC, bore anguished witness to this crisis in his report of August 1967. He took issue with the new theological views which call into question "the reality of God, the Father of our Lord Jesus Christ, as it is revealed to the eye of faith in the Bible". He challenged the charges of conservatism and obscurantism that have been made by the German school of de-mythologization and the American death-of-God theologians: "If it be true, so be it," he said, "because the ecumenical movement will ever and always depend on the transcendent God who has been revealed in his Son, our Lord." The new theology threatened to subvert the unity of biblical revelation, the foundations of ecclesiology in the New Testament, and hence the very basis for the WCC. It

---

[1] This author followed closely the proceedings of the Uppsala Convention. For additional information, see my article, "L'Assemblée d'Upsal," in *Rythmes du Monde* [2] (1968).

was Dr. Visser 't Hooft who had raised the first cry of alarm a year earlier (Geneva 1966).[2]

Impressed by these early warnings, the organizers of the Uppsala convention prepared for an all-out offensive from the new theology. The offensive did not materialize, for two obvious but different reasons. On the one hand, sociological concerns, backed up by the insistent challenges of young people who had little interest left in theology, channeled the outlook toward the problems of man and the world. On the other hand, the strong pressure of the Orthodox members (now the largest single confession in the WCC), supported by the Catholic observers and guests,[3] had a surprisingly decisive effect on the eventual orientation of the theological program. The report of Section I on "The Holy Spirit and the Catholicity of the Church", for example, was fashioned on a trinitarian base. The expected offensive never took place. And we can honestly say that time and again the tendency toward an excessively functional theology was offset by a healthy stress on the ontological values of the *Credo*.

Does this mean that the dread specters have vanished into thin air? Alas, no. The crisis remains, and it will come to a head again, sooner or later, insofar as the texts of a convention are not normative. It still rages in the Catholic Church, too, despite the *aggiornamento* of Vatican Council II. That is why I feel obliged to stress this point: our first ecumenical duty is to redouble our efforts to master this crisis.

To point up the urgency of a problem, however, is not to solve it. Let me just note that several approaches could be used. The first would start with a profession of faith, modeled on the ternary rhythm of the *Credo*. The *Credo* provides us with a certain analogical knowledge of the three divine Persons, through the works which tradition attributes to them "by appropriation". Let no one laugh at this idea: this classic work, more courageous than it may appear, would be of great utility today.

[2] See also my article, "La grâce de l'oecuménisme aujourd'hui," in *Nouv. Rev. Théol.* (May 1968), pp. 517-24.

[3] It is to be noted that six Catholic theologians were accredited as members of the Faith and Constitution Commission.

But it would be more expedient, I feel, to start with man and proceed inductively, as the *New Dutch Catechism* does. Note the main lines of this fine introduction to the faith: the mystery of existence, the way to Christ, the Son of Man, the way of Christ, the way to the end. At each major stage, we would try to isolate the mystery of God's transcendence and man. This approach would be more satisfactory to the contemporary mentality, for it fits in with the theology of salvation history.

All along the road, of course, we shall encounter the byways of our denominational differences. But this is not the moment to dwell on them. The important thing is to rediscover the road itself *together*. This journey side by side will create mutual confidence between us. Or, to put it better, it will create between us a transparency that will help us to return later to our denominational conflicts, and we shall be surprised to find how the complexion of these conflicts has changed. This would be a new approach, one to which we are not accustomed, but one which would certainly be more comfortable. In any case, we shall have overcome the crisis of faith through prayer and the grace of the Lord.

## The Problems of Eucharistic Communion

An impatient desire for intercommunion (between Catholics and Protestants, and between Orthodox Christians and Protestants) is welling up like a tidal wave, as shown, for example, at the meetings of young people at Taizé these past years. The proposal to have perpetual prayer at the crypt has happily transformed this "violent impatience" into "zealous patience", to use the prior's words, but it has not resolved the problem. Then there is the intercelebration of Pentecost in Paris, which has been censured by the hierarchy despite its alleged prophetic significance.

As might have been expected, the tidal wave broke with full force on Uppsala during the convention. Catholics, including priests, took part in the communion services of the Swedish Church. Secret services of intercelebration took place. A group of Protestants and Catholics (both laymen and priests) resolved to practice intercommunion *henceforth*. All these actions are reprehensible, and they could only upset the serenity of the debate.

There was indeed a debate during three long sessions of the Faith and Constitution Committee. It concerned a text that had been prepared on this problem. Arguments and protests were heard from different groups. A group of Catholic and Protestant students already considered themselves as members of the united Church of Christ (the Church of Tomorrow). In perfectly good faith, they claimed the right to commune at the same table, in either denominational Church. If this right were denied them, they would leave their traditional Churches.

More balanced and competent was the oft repeated demand of some Protestant clergymen, which had already been cited by Max Thurian in *Le pain unique*. They noted that Protestant and Catholic experts already share a set of values on the general doctrine of the eucharist. Couldn't this consensus be deepened by allowing them to intercommune, at least during ecumenical encounters? Properly guided, this could be a means of grace that would help to achieve full unity. (There is a hint of this solution in the conciliar *Decree on Ecumenism*.) Finally, some noted that intercommunion was already a *fait accompli*, and that it was high time for theologians to find a justification for it.

In the end, the Orthodox and Catholic theologians (who shall remain nameless) declined to carry through with the question, and no progress was made. The Orthodox were totally adamant: only an explicit profession of the Orthodox faith could allow communion at the Orthodox altar.[4] The Catholic theologians had varying views and were more open to the demands of the young ("who have their two feet in the present and cannot grasp the imperatives of tradition"); they were opposed to outright refusal, but they left this problem open because "it has not yet

---

[4] Only Prof. G. Klinger (Warsaw) left the question open. It is true, he noted, that intercommunion can only be practiced within the precincts of the true Church. But what are the limits of the Church today? Vatican Council II itself did not give an answer to that question, so I shall not say yes or no.

ripened". My impression was that these responses were conditioned by the pervading atmosphere of independence, not to say open rebellion, and by the extremely heterogeneous nature of the audience. They were not worked out fully and carefully enough.

So what was to be done? A basis of agreement had to be sought on another level. Max Thurian led the way, asking that the invited Churches, at the very least, approve the London proposal of 1952 on "open communion". The London declaration asks something of Churches whose discipline forbids their members to approach the communion rail of other Churches (the Protestant Churches, in effect): that they agree to receive at their communion rail, in certain ecumenical circumstances, their separated brethren who come to receive the body of Christ from them. The idea is that these Christians thereby demonstrate that they already feel associated with them in the communion of the universal Church.

It was also Max Thurian who pointed out that this practice could be justified by a broad interpretation of Rome's *Ecumenical Handbook,* and everyone knows that some Roman Catholic bishops have permitted this practice in specific cases.[5] Couldn't Roman Catholic and Orthodox discipline be stretched that far? If we could not have a reciprocal gesture, could we not open the door that much at least? Again the response was *negative.*

I should like to dwell on this specific point for a moment, because I believe that such an overture is now possible. When my Anglican or Lutheran friend presents himself to me at the altar rail, he wants me to give Christ to him. He knows Christ is present there, and the theological explanation I may give for the mode of Christ's presence is of relatively minor importance to him. (However important it may be in fact, it is of secondary importance in this specific situation.) What is certain is that he does not refuse it; he simply makes a *positive* act of faith in the eucharist, and he does not destroy or restrict this act by any

---

[5] We have it on the best authority that Patriarch Athenagoras broke the eucharistic bread with members of a Protestant pilgrimage to Istanbul —a courageous exception!

negative act of heresy. On my side, this gesture of welcome could pave the way for an explanation, in biblical terms, of the value and objectivity of the Lord's memorial—an explanation which we both could accept and come together on.

Thus, something which has already been authorized (but only rarely) in specific circumstances could become the precedent for a broader discipline in certain ecumenical situations to be decided upon. Need we say that we are excluding any and all proselytizing contexts? We are simply trying to meet a Protestant request halfway—a request that has already been sanctioned by the London Conference.

This whole matter of receiving our Christian brothers at our communion rail came across to me during the theological debates at Uppsala. But those debates failed to consider the preliminary question of the *ministry*. It is not that the theologians there were unaware of the issue; the impatience of their audience probably influenced their approach. Yet I was shocked and dismayed by their failure to step back and examine the question. The possibility of mutually recognizing our separate ministries is under serious discussion, as Volume 34 of *Concilium* proves. They should have mentioned this and developed the key points. However, a rapid poll indicated that most of them had not even read these articles!

I am not going to reexamine the same issue in this volume of *Concilium*. I would merely refer the reader to volume 34. I would also call the reader's attention to a paper of George Tavard, *Signification du ministère protestant,* presented at the Conference of the Consultation on Church Union (Detroit 1968). It contains some very suggestive remarks: "It is not apostolic succession that makes the Church catholic; it is the catholicity of the Church that guarantees apostolic succession; thus the validity [of the Church's ministry] could disappear at one point in history, to reappear later." In this connection, the Uppsala text on "The Holy Spirit and the Catholicity of the Church" opens the door wide to our hopes. We must work together in this direction with courage and boldness.

## Rome in the World Council of Churches

This idea, unthinkable a few years ago, took a decisive step forward at Uppsala. The prime reason was the address of Father Robert Tucci, S.J. on "The Roman Catholic Church and the World Council of Churches". Father Tucci is the editor of *Civiltà Cattolica,* an official organ of the Holy See. He set about the task of removing the obstacles that might prevent Rome from seeking membership in the WCC, and even though he spoke in his own name, the import of his words were plain to all. Father Tucci convinced the assembly that there was no longer any major obstacle to Rome's membership.

No longer can the WCC send out a platonic, no-risk invitation to Rome. Now Rome, by actively applying for membership, could pose all sorts of new and delicate problems to the WCC. To begin with, there is the ticklish question of equitable representation. How can the WCC take in a worldwide Church, comprising more than half of Christendom, without upsetting the already delicate balance between the Orthodox Churches and the Protestant Churches? Would it not call for a total reorganization in structure? It is a noble and well-intentioned challenge, and the WCC faced it squarely. The decision was that if Rome did apply for membership, the WCC would not reject it. There is still time to work on the problem, because Rome's membership could not be ratified before the next convention.

I am not going to weigh the pros and cons of this possibility here. Some are alarmed by it, feeling that the already existing sideline collaboration between Rome and Geneva is excellent and sufficient. But the problems confronting man and the world are enormous in scope, and marginal collaboration will never allow for the full effectiveness to be realized from full membership.

In saying this, I do not foresee any direct advance on the doctrinal level. Membership in the WCC would be in line with the bilateral and multilateral talks now going on between Rome and the other great Churches and Federations. We would have a chance to formulate decisions of worldwide scope, decisions which must be elaborated jointly from a common center if they are to be fully effective. That center, by supposition, cannot be Rome.

And what about the modest ecumenist who is not privy to the secrets of the gods? What can he do? He can do a great deal. Through his talks and articles, he can mold the opinion of Church leaders and the Christian people. The latter have grasped the grand ideals of Uppsala far better than we dared to expect. He can also channel the thrust of Unity Week in this direction, especially if he is a priest. Let us hope that all Christians will perseveringly pray for an outpouring of the Spirit on Rome and Geneva, so that this great grace may be granted by him "who makes all things new".

---

A Protestant Viewpoint
Heinz Zahrnt, Hamburg, West Germany

The answer to the question posed here depends upon an even more basic question: How does the theologian see his task, and how ready is he to take it seriously?

Courage implies that a man has a certain attitude and outlook toward the future. The courageous man is one who does not desperately hang on to past tradition, hoary with the endorsement of countless generations, but who faces the present situation and stays open to the things he may encounter. Unlike the author of Ecclesiastes, the courageous man believes that there can be something new under the sun. Such courage, I believe, is to be found among some theologians in both great Churches of Western Christendom.

In attending the discussions now taking place in Catholic and Protestant circles, I have come to notice something. Time and again I have found it hard to tell whether a Catholic or a Protestant was speaking. And when I have addressed an audience of Catholic theologians, I have quite forgotten where I was during the question and answer period. The questions could have come from a Protestant group. This suggests to me that the critical lines of division in present-day theology cut across denominational lines rather than running parallel to them.

The critical question is how theology sees itself and approaches its task. Is it ready to confront the present situation, and to rework its talk of God so that it does truly relate to God and the world? Or will it close its eyes to the contemporary situation, so that its talk of God says nothing about the real God and the real world? Here again, it seems to me, a noticeable change in attitude is taking place among theologians in both Churches. To put it somewhat oversimplified terms, they are moving from "established certitude" to "dialogue".

## From Proofs to Proclamation

For a long time in the Church, it was felt that the theologian's profession was to stand guard over the purity of Church doctrine. The basic outlook was the same in the Catholic Church and the Protestant Church, even though there were many differences in specifics. Both Churches cherished the same a-historical notion of truth: Truth was something which could be established and fixed with certitude, both in content and in time. Man could come to know the objective truth, and he was obliged to hand it down to later generations unchanged. Stress was put on the continuing identity of tradition, not on its variability through history.

This notion of truth had an impact on the way theology was conceived and practiced. To a large extent, it was a field for experts, and God became the province of professionals and specialists. The experts traded their findings with each other, to be sure, but it was a closed trading arrangement confined to one's own denomination and one's fellow experts. The same held true for both "orthodox" theology and "historico-critical" theology, except that the latter dealt more with historical concerns than with dogmatic points. Theologians reclined under the tree of knowledge in small coteries, sampling and sharing its fruit, while other Adams and Eves had to carry on the affairs of everyday life in the sweat of their brow.

The task of standing guard over the purity of Church doctrine introduced a note of strained anxiety and unhappiness into the work of theologians. Few theologians of past centuries could really feel that Wisdom *delighted to play* among men in the fields of this world. After reading many theological books, even those of "modern" theologians, I get a picture of two men arguing heatedly at the top of some cathedral about some minor architectural point; meanwhile, down on the ground, ordinary people have no idea what the fuss is all about, and they walk away shaking their heads.

I find it hard to believe that the whole matter of God is as complicated as we theologians often make it. We cannot justify the intricacies of our theology by pointing to the hiddenness of God. God is hidden in mystery, indeed, but he is never complicated. The complexity of our theology is in direct opposition to God's revelation. By it we go against the will of God, as it is revealed to us in the Bible from first page to last. For the Bible tells us that God is out looking for man, trying to communicate and share knowledge with him.

In all God's words and deeds, as they are portrayed for us in the Bible, we find the same orientation and thrust. God, in his love, is looking for man. He wants to start a dialogue with mankind, and that is why he has addressed his truth to men. Whether the overzealous seekers of truth like it or not, God's truth is directed toward an *end,* and that end is mankind.

The transmission of God's revelation in the Bible is patterned after its dialogic character. It is handed down as "kerygma". Biblical tradition deals with some specific reality that did take place in the past, but it does not treat it as some established piece of dry historical information. It is proclaimed in faith, and thus brought up into the present. And the express purpose of this proclamation is to beget further proclamation and to arouse faith anew. What else can this mean but that God's dialogue with mankind is carried on in the Church's proclamation?

From the dialogic character of biblical tradition, it naturally follows that the Christian kerygma shows variety and multiplicity. Proclamation requires that the speaker adapt himself to the situation of the listener, although he cannot wholly abstract from his own situation. It follows, then, that in the New Testament the one revelation of God's love in Jesus Christ is attested to in a variety of ways—some seeming to contradict others.

We could put it this way: In the New Testament there is only *one Christ,* but there are *many christologies.* None of us has the one Christ; each of us does have his own christology. If we realized that fact, we could spare ourselves much time, energy and argument in theology. There would still be stumbling blocks in theology, but there would be no theological chagrin.

God's revelation is the starting point for all theology, and this revelation took place as a dialogue rather than a theophany. Furthermore, the biblical transmission of revelation took the form of kerygma, and the biblical kerygma forms the source of all theology. Now if all this is true, then the character of theology is determined in advance. It must be more dialogue than thesis and proof; it must be more hermeneutics than dogmatics.

This requirement is made all the more urgent for theology by another fact. In our day the Enlightenment has finally broken in with full force on the faith and on theology. The most decisive aspect of the Enlightenment was that all traditional authorities up to that time were no longer taken for granted; they became problematical. This transformation, which previously had affected all the aspects of man's existence, is now taking place in the realm of faith and theology. The nature of authority is undergoing radical change.

No longer do the tenets of the Christian faith possess self-evident authority. They, too, must demonstrate their authority over and over again by proving that they are intelligible and persuasive to contemporary men. The time of simple theses and catechism answers is over. Today men also want to know the why and the wherefore of the Christian faith. Does this not mean that theology simply has to be dialogue today?

## Courage in Theology

Theological dialogue, of its very nature, always has to involve three participants. Theologians must talk to each other, and to the world. Just as the world is always present in any real conversation about God, so Geneva and Rome must consider the fate of Niniveh and Babylon in their conversations with one another. A dialogue with the world must be part and parcel of their dialogue with each other. And today, theology's dialogue with the world takes precedence.

In revealing his truth, God stepped into the world and tried to reach man by means of an *aggiornamento*. In like manner, we must relate God's truth to the locale in which it is being proclaimed, if it is to be comprehensible. Our primary task today is to make theology human, even as God once became man. God's truth always stands within a specific historical horizon; it is framed in a specific time and place. But do we theologians in both confessions really know what hour has struck?

Today we are faced with a "monetary crisis" of enormous proportions in theology. All the great words and images and concepts of the Bible, which we have taken for granted so long, have become worthless paper money in the eyes of our contemporaries. And many of us sit protectively on a pile of this paper money, refusing to believe that it has been devalued.

Our talk about God is pious prattle or ideological fantasy if it is not suffused with the concrete experience of practical reality. This is the thrust of life today: Only what is real and available to man's experience seems credible today. In our reflection and our talk about God, we must come to appreciate and to show how we encounter the reality of God in our real life and the real world. We must come to appreciate that God is "real", and then talk about his reality in a comprehensible and credible way. We must make clear to others how much the life of a believer depends upon the reality of God. If man does not discover the connection between the reality of God and the reality of the world, then God will remain an authoritative dictate, and faith in him will be something on the remote borders of real life.

In the future, talk about God can only survive if it is tied up with talk about the world. The wondrous works of God can only survive if they are tied up with the great events of history. If we do not talk about God in these terms, then we shall be like a pedantic antiquarian trying to sell ancient clay pots as modern kitchenware. Our audience will be rather small.

No one can manage the new task alone. No longer can one man, one institution, or one ecclesiastical magisterium claim to possess the truth about God and to dole it out under the protective mantle of infallibility. Today the principle of teamwork also applies to the realm of divine truth. Two men, working together, have a better chance of finding truth than one man alone. Therefore, they engage in dialogue with one another.

Now this presupposes that each side is prepared to check out the elements of truth it claims to possess, and to reject them if they prove to be false. Readiness to emend and correct the truth we start with is what distinguishes dialogue from declamation. In the latter, the prepared text lies open before the speaker. In the former, there is no prepared text at the start; it takes shape as the discussion proceeds, and no one knows in advance how it will turn out.

If we view the theological discussions taking place with the love and humor that are demanded, we shall realize that all of us are talking about the same divine revelation. We differ in what we have to say about it. Each person speaks from his own standpoint. All address each other as living men of flesh and blood, who have their own distinctive traits, their own backlog of tradition, their own viewpoints, and their own store of experiences. We view God's unique truth from different perspectives.

Now this does not come down to "relativism", nor does it mean that we give up or betray the quest for real truth. On the contrary, it is the diversity of standpoints that drives us into discussion. Since we all are talking about the same divine revelation, we can respect each other's opinion, but we cannot leave each other in self-satisfied peace. We must talk to each other, and listen to each other. And so dialogue is born.

Indeed, such dialogue is possible only if there are different viewpoints to begin with. When there are no points of disagreement, then theology is a choir of unanimous voices, and the voice out of tune belongs to a heretic. Dialogue comes to an end, and we are left with a multi-part monologue. In such a case, truth comes to an end also, and a false authority expropriates the authority of truth itself. For truth is to be found among men only in the living process of mutual discussion, only in the joint quest for truth.

What courageous action can the theologian take to further ecumenical understanding? He can pursue the task of theology courageously! We theologians excuse ourselves when we occasionally say something bold and daring. We hurriedly add that we have been speaking "off the record", or that we have not "thought it through". Would that we had the courage to say bold things more often. Experience suggests that we often speak our best thoughts "off the record".

# How Can Ecumenical Understanding Be Furthered by the Bishop?

A CATHOLIC VIEWPOINT
Léon-Joseph Cardinal Suenens, Mechelen, Belgium

I have been asked for a reply to the question: What can a bishop do to promote ecumenical understanding in a real fashion. It is thus a case of a bishop as such, abstracting from whatever is not proper to him. It seems to me that the best procedure in attempting to outline a reply would be to distinguish what concerns the bishop as a member of the episcopal college and what pertains to him as head of a local Church.

## I

### THE BISHOP ON THE LEVEL OF THE UNIVERSAL CHURCH

Everyone knows—and His Holiness Pope Paul VI has openly stated—that the major obstacle to ecumenical understanding is the dogma of the primacy of the pope, as defined by Vatican Council I. The main objection to this primacy is the assertion that in practice it eliminates episcopal collegiality or reduces it below the vital minimum. Vatican Council II—first by its mere existence and then by its action and texts—has highlighted the inalienable role of the episcopal body with and under Peter. But a Council text—no matter how important—is after all only a text; it lives solely through its translation into the concrete, its "Sitz im Leben". The Orthodox, Anglican and Protestant world is particularly interested in seeing the manner in which the bishops will translate this collegial attitude into actions.

At the close of the Council, Professor Outler, observer of the Methodist Church at the Council, wrote in an American magazine that the test of our ecumenical sincerity will be the implementation of episcopal collegiality at the very heart of the Church. And even before the Council, Dr. Ramsey, archbishop of Canterbury, had written the following significant lines in his book *The Gospel and the Catholic Church:* "The discovery of its precise functions [i.e., of the primacy] will come not by discussion of the Petrine claims in isolation but by the recovery everywhere of the body's organic life, with its bishops, presbyters and people. In this body Peter will find his due place, and ultimate reunion is hastened not by the pursuit of 'the papal controversy' but by the quiet growth of the organic life of every part of Christendom." [1]

This is true especially of the bishop who is co-responsible with the pope for the life of the Church. An episcopal co-responsibility that is lived and carried to its logical and concrete consequences is, in today's Church, an eminently ecumenical service. If we desire to eliminate the "major obstacle" from the road that leads to visible unity, the primacy of the pope—which is contested by no Catholic—must appear within the balanced and complementary framework proclaimed by the Council. But how can this common concern be translated into life? A Council is doubtless a spectacular expression of this co-responsibility: its mere existence has led to the disappearance of a good many fears or prejudices, and its actions have even contributed strongly to marking out the path toward ecumenism. But a Council is rare, and Vatican Council III is not yet on the horizon. Hence, the question arises for the present: What can be done by the bishop on the level of the universal Church?

[1] A. M. Ramsey, *The Gospel and the Catholic Church* (London, 1955), p. 228.

My answer would be: he can fully assume his proper responsibility in the institutions which Vatican Council II has created, and take advantage of the possibilities for active presence that have been opened up at Rome.

This collaboration on the part of bishops finds a completely natural place in the new organ created as the fruit of Vatican Council II: the synod of bishops. A first experience took place in October 1967, bringing together at Rome some 200 bishops of the universal Church, representing their respective episcopal conferences. On the subject of the synod we have expressed a few reflections in our book *La coresponsabilité dans l'Eglise d'aujourd'hui*.[2] Here we will simply note that this experience which was timid and groping but positive as a whole should enable us to derive important improvements for the future, if we want the synod of bishops to enjoy a truly collegial role.

For example, episcopal co-responsibility must enter into play even in the preparations for the synod. This implies that episcopal conferences can collaborate in the very composition of the agenda and give their opinion of the "argumenta" to be treated in order of urgency and pastoral importance. Well before the opening of a synod, there should be a real exchange between the "center" and the "periphery", not merely concerning the agenda, but also concerning the working mechanism of the synod, for the future avoidance of tiresome monologues and to the profit of true dialogue. How then can we refrain from hoping that experts in discussion techniques can help to draw a maximum efficiency from these meetings that are so rich in potentialities?

As for the members of the synod, such as we have known them, there is room for clarifying certain situations. For example, as much as the presence of the prefects of the Roman Congregations would seem desirable, their role as executive power of the Holy See would militate against giving them a deliberative voice on the day when the synod should be in session. The reason for this is the desire not to frustrate the full play of collegiality

[2] Cf. L. J. Suenens, *La coresponsabilite dans l'Eglise d'aujourd'hui* (Bruges, 1968), pp. 80-86.

which is exercised above all by the representatives of episcopal conferences.

Similarly, we do not see the reason why experts, as was the case, should be members of the synod. This is in no way to assert—just the opposite—that their presence is not highly to be desired. They could play a very important role in the synodal commissions which we believe are indispensable for ensuring effective labor; the setting up of these commissions was too haphazard according to the established system. We could go on at length in listing the desirable improvements concerning the procedure for debates, voting, etc. As a matter of fact, episcopal conferences have been invited to suggest improvement in view of later synods. But here it is sufficient for us merely to indicate the eminently ecumenical interest of a less passive and more actively collaborative interest on the part of episcopal conferences in the labors of the synod.

Everything that accentuates and improves the dialogue between the "center" and "periphery" is of capital importance. It is in putting into practice the pluralism of particular Churches that the central unity stands out better and is deepened: uniformity is not synonymous with true unity, any more than conformism is the test of obedience. We must live the communion of local Churches at the highest level, in the heart of the Catholic Church. In so doing, we will pave the way for the visible communion of the Christian Churches at the heart of the one Church, which is the very hope of ecumenism.

Another opportunity for collegial breakthrough is presented by the recent reform of the Roman Curia. Besides the internationalization which offers very fine possibilities in this sense, the Motu Proprio "Pro comperto sane" of August 6, 1967 provides for the presence of seven residential bishops at the center of each Congregation. The principle of this participation is a felicitous one, and the practice will yield its good results. Everything will depend here also on the truly collegial spirit which will be shown by the designated bishops. Formerly, foreign residential cardinals were members of one or other Congregation. In this capacity they had the right to attend plenary assemblies when these coincided with their trips to Rome. But everyone knows that this participation is more theoretical than practical.

On this point it is necessary to rethink the working methods of the Congregations so that the contribution of foreign bishops can be truly valuable and effective. It will be very important to provide for real continuity in this collaboration during the course of the whole year—that is, in the intervals between meetings. Much will depend on the vigorous manner in which the bishops associated with the work of the Congregations will take the initiative and, where necessary, defend pastoral positions which are not those of the Congregations themselves.

In order that a dialogue may be effective and fruitful, there must be debate on preliminary and basic questions. It is useless to discuss questions of details after options have already been taken if the very presuppositions of a problem have not previously been examined with complete freedom. If such examinations appear radical in certain cases, they will seem all the more necessary. The success of common efforts is had only at this price. The experience of the preparatory commissions for the Council shows to what extent there can be a shift from the juridical preoccupations of a Congregation to the pastoral concerns of bishops actively engaged in pastoral life. Compare, for example, the primitive schema prepared by a Congregation and submitted to the preparatory commission of bishops and the text voted on: there is a world of difference between the two.

Undoubtedly, all of this directly concerns only a certain number of bishops called to Rome by designation of their colleagues or direct nomination. But through these intermediaries each bishop can collaborate in emphasizing collegial responsibility and thus implicitly fostering ecumenical harmony. Everyone must tell himself that the Council is not yet completed and in one sense is only beginning. Life is more eloquent than declarations, and everyone knows—following Zeno—that nothing demonstrates movement better than progress.

## II
### The Bishop at the Heart of the Particular Church

However, this kind of ecumenism is not taking place only in Rome; it is going on at the heart of each particular Church, which is not merely a part of the universal Church but the very Church of Christ present under another mode. The Council has emphasized the co-responsibility of all the members of the People of God. This emphasis is eminently ecumenical. The Orthodox world attaches the greatest importance to this communion of all in the bosom of the People of God. The "sobornost" is a living reality at the heart of Orthodoxy. On its side, the Protestant world has placed the accent on the priesthood of all the baptized and on the active role of each of the faithful. Despite the differences which still remain on these points among the Churches— less in what is affirmed than in what is denied—a convergence is taking shape in attitudes and deeds. The bishop, more than anyone else, is called upon to put into practice in the daily life of his own Church the active and converging collaboration of all: priests, deacons, religious and laity. This implies another way of exercising episcopal authority.

Much is said about the present crisis of authority, and it is real, but we believe the manner of exercising authority is more of a crisis. Formerly, authority appeared above all as a juridical power of command; today, authority is conceived chiefly as a service rendered to the community by making the effort of all converge toward the common end. If the bishop appears as the isolated head of his presbyterium and his people, he retards not only the evolution taking place within the heart of the Church, but he also hinders the progress of ecumenism. On the level of both the universal and the local Church, the image of authority experienced will be a *decisive* factor in the harmony of Churches. We need merely think of John XXIII who simply by his manner of exercising authority caused ecumenism to take great strides, laying to rest a good many prejudices. Paul VI, a "pilgrim on the move" to Jerusalem or to Constantinople, evokes other images which themselves give cause for hope and prophetism.

It has been said that ideas are stronger than armies; nowadays, in the century of the visual, images can have a nuclear force. Each bishop is called upon at his level to shatter a certain conventional image of the bishop of yesterday and substitute the rejuvenated image of the post-conciliar bishop. We are emerging from a long era of juridicism, legalism, and at times even—it must be admitted—"talmudism". The absolute monarch type of authority is in the process of disappearing and giving way to a new type of authority based on multiple and diversified collaboration rooted in the whole.

Of course, we must not substitute for a juridicism "from superior to inferior" another juridicism "from inferior to superior"; the latter would be as harmful as the former and betray true coresponsibility by abusively expressing it in terms of parlementarianism. The Christian variety of "participation" is too much a reality of faith to be reduced to our single human schemas and sociological categories. Ecclesial communion must be respected in all its complexity and complementariety; the bishop has the eminent task of situating himself at its heart and animating it.

In promoting this active communion in theological faith, hope and charity at the heart of his own Church, the bishop fulfills the primordial requirements of Vatican Council II. In so doing, he responds to what "the Spirit says to the Churches" in the hour of ecumenism.

———————

A PROTESTANT VIEWPOINT
Johannes Lilje, Hannover, West Germany

Two presuppositions underlie the question posed here. The first is that the bishop's duty in this area is obviously not to be identified with that of the community member or the community pastor; it involves something more. The question reveals an awareness that the episcopal office is an ecumenical office. The bishop must always keep the whole of Christendom in mind. Ecumenical responsibility is an unrelinquishable element of the episcopal office rightly understood.

The second presupposition is that the bishop must do something bold and courageous. He does not fulfill his duty completely if he simply carries on the traditions of the past. The bishop must do his part to bring the Churches together, and they can only come together if they resolutely move forward. When the question of ecumenical understanding is put forward seriously, it must focus on the *tasks* placed on Christendom by the world in which we live. It is not necessary to say expressly that the mission of the Church should not be simply surrendered to the world, but it is meaningless to talk about ecumenical obligations if we are not determined to face the world of today as it really is.

### Courage in Thought

The first obligation of the bishop is to be bold and courageous in his thinking. He must involve himself in the task of mastering the spiritual and intellectual problems which Christendom faces today. Much has been said about changing social structures. Everyone is aware of the revolutionary changes taking place in our mental picture of the world. And, finally, there are elemental historical forces pushing us forward toward the future: for example, the whole thrust of the "third world" or the "underdeveloped nations". Some questions are not so abstract and academic as those relating to our changing intellectual ideas. Some have to do with such basic, concrete issues as the gap between rich and poor, the resistance of conservative blocs to change, and the impatient rush of revolutionary forces toward a new world order.

The intellectual mastery of our present situation is itself something which calls for a high degree of intellectual courage. We cannot familiarize ourselves with the essential processes at work today if Christianity avoids facing up to the new questions confronting us. One of the high points of the fourth convention of the World Council of Churches in Uppsala was the lecture by Barbara Ward (Lady Jackson). In her address, she brilliantly tackled the theme of the convention: "Behold, I make all things new." She pointed out that Christianity would be able to proclaim this message to the world only if it were ready to accept and approve the new things that have already taken place or that are now in progress. She pointed to the new policies in the areas of national development and world agriculture, suggesting that the activities of the secular world had far outstripped the concern and initiative of the Christian Churches.

Within our Churches there is too much traditionalism. They are not courageous enough to tackle the new tasks with enthusiasm. In recent months we have had shameful examples of their inability to tackle and solve the peculiar problems posed by contemporary political structure and policies. What could we do, and what did we do, to counteract the genocidal events in Biafra? The starvation of countless human beings was clearly and unmistakably a human problem, so we should have been able to find some way of solving it effectively and bypassing the political strictures involved. But we didn't. The Biafran problem reveals not only the political impotence of the big powers, but also the sinful inaction of Christians. Almost three decades after World War II, we still have not managed to develop political machinery that could step into such crises and work energetically toward their solution.

This is what I am referring to when I talk about Christendom's obligation to display intellectual and spiritual courage. And here the bishop has a specific leadership role to play. Ordinarily he is in a better position to get an overall view of the situation than is the local pastor or his community. Consequently, he has an obligation to pass along his knowledge to others—and I am talking about something more than informational press releases. It takes courage to break down the curtain of silence that is maintained by the guardians of the status quo.

This intellectual and spiritual courage should operate in two spheres. It should take action in the world at large, and within the precincts of the Church herself.

*In the world at large,* it is not always easy to clarify and explain the great problems confronting Christendom to all those who approach the Church. They all are looking for answers, but they expect different things from the Church. For some, the Church is too political; for others, she does not show enough political courage. For some, she goes overboard in her concern for the developing nations; for others, she does not show enough strength and commitment to these world problems.

In such a situation, a bishop must have the courage to plead the Church's case clearly and unequivocally, without courting popularity or the favor of the public. He will speak with wisdom and kindness, but frequently he will have to lay it on the line and upset the smugness and complacency of the bourgeois mentality —and that takes courage.

It will probably take just as much courage for him to speak out *within the precincts of the Church,* to drive home these important tasks to his own Church community and its local pastors. Here, too, he must learn to disregard the quest for public popularity and official approval. He must clearly spell out the present tasks to his community, and impress upon it the urgency of confronting the contemporary world and its problems. He cannot fail in this duty.

Around what, specifically, is this intellectual courage oriented? Let us consider a few examples.

To begin with, there is the difficult and many-faceted field of theology—a critical battleground today. The present tensions in this field, ranging from bedrock fundamentalism to a dissatisfaction with all the traditional presentations of the Christian faith, represent a real test for Christendom. No bishop can avoid this problem. He will display his intellectual courage by facing up to those who inform him that his God is dead, or that the traditional formulations of the Christian faith are no longer relevant because they do not fit in with the real demands of present-day society.

To be sure, he will not be ready to agree that God is dead, or that the word "God" can no longer be explained in terms that have real meaning. He will regard any attempt to replace authentic Christian dogmas with socio-political ties as hopeless abstractionism. But he will not do this by retreating behind the protective cover of traditional dogmatic formulas. For these formulas could well turn out to be straw men, unable to withstand the first assault of contemporary questions.

The bishop will have to think through these debates with energy and sympathy. This is particularly important. Many members of the Christian community will simply withdraw from these discussions, firmly believing that they are thereby preserving and protecting their Christian faith. But a bishop would be derelict in his duty if he did not help his community to face up to these questions bravely. One of the demands of leadership is to lead his community into the fray; he must show them that true Christian courage means opening up to these questions, believing that God is greater than our hearts (1 Jn. 3, 20) and our intellectual capacities, and realizing that these debates and discussions cannot be avoided by the Christian community of today.

The clock of Church history cannot be stopped, nor is it the bishop's duty to champion a false passivity or traditionalism. His true task, obviously enough, demands a high degree of intellectual strength and a strong faith. He must support and think through the "coexistence of vertical and horizontal lines of sight in theological debate" (Dr. W. A. Visser 't Hooft), for this tension in perspectives must be maintained.

The duty of the bishop, however, goes far beyond this commitment to theology. In many cases he must take some concrete action as well.

## Courage in Action

We find situations where discussion has gone as far as it can go. All the arguments have been presented, the pros and cons have been analyzed, and the mind can go no further. The limits of rational elucidation have been reached.

In such a situation, it may be the bishop's duty to step in personally and move the discussion forward by a bold step. In this way he may help to promote ecumenical understanding and joint religious services among different denominations, or to solve some socio-political problem that could not be settled theoretically on traditional grounds.

Let us be precise as to what we mean here, for two wrong detours are possible. The first detour would be a purely individual sortie of a rash nature. It is a relatively easy thing to do, but only rarely does it represent a truly prophetic action that cannot be ignored. Ordinarily, no matter how spectacular and well publicized it is, the act proves to be ineffectual and without practical impact. It is not often in Church history that the revolutionary action of an individual has launched a real movement, so we should not be overawed by the shrill cries of the overenthusiastic.

The second wrong detour would be to avoid coming to any decision, to keep going back over the intellectual theory without ever arriving at a personal commitment. A bishop will avoid both extremes, but his personal actions will be tempered by the knowledge that his action will have an impact on the whole Church. This can help him to forestall many misunderstandings and misinterpretations, and it will make him realize clearly the obligation imposed on him.

Such personal initiatives by a bishop can do much to move forward a deadlocked dialogue. Even Protestants are aware of the example set by John XXIII in this area. His personal initiatives surmounted many theological, canonical and organizational barriers, and their practical consequences were great.

There is another area to be considered here. What can the bishop do, *in his everyday activity,* to further ecumenical understanding in a proper way? Put simply, he can promote openness between human beings, the openness which is necessary if Christians of different denominations are to encounter each other and those who can no longer regard themselves as members of Christendom.

To be sure, it takes a certain measure of courage to seek

dialogue with today's Marxists, atheists and nihilists—real open-ended dialogue that does not prejudge the other party in advance. And it seems to me that two of the noblest traits of a real, living Christian way of life are these: (1) the intellectual courage to face up to new, unfamiliar and difficult questions time and again; (2) absolute freedom from prejudice and prejudgment.

There is no need for us to dwell on the harm which prejudice has done to mankind. The vise of prejudice has done much to prevent true community among human beings. Authentic Christian behavior demands that we put aside the clichés and stereotypes with which we approach each other, that we leave no room for our personal prejudices, and that we show as much openness as possible in our dealings with one another. This would be the right way for us to exemplify the brotherhood of man, and to show the other person that he, too, is God's creature.

Human dignity is not a Christian privilege. Wherever this dignity is seriously threatened, the Christian must stand up for the downtrodden and oppressed, and this is almost always an act of great personal and Christian courage. Today, in Latin America, hundreds of bishops and priests are under police surveillance. That tells us one way in which such courage can be practiced in socio-political life.

It is the bishop's particular duty, when circumstances demand it, to perform these courageous acts in such a clear and unmistakable way that he teaches his community the meaning of obedience to God's Word and God's commandment. In the 16th century, one of the bravest Reformers tried to rouse his bewildered community. Zwingli had this to say to his beleaguered people: "For God's sake, do something courageous." This is not bad advice for any bishop who wants to live up to his ecumenical obligations today.

# How Can Ecumenical Understanding Be Furthered by the Pope?

AN ANGLICAN VIEWPOINT
Hugh Montefiore, Cambridge, England

I am an Anglican priest, and one who looks at the Church of Rome from outside may perhaps be in a better position than Roman Catholics to sympathize with the present pope. The Anglican Archbishop Davidson, when challenged about his leadership, is said to have replied: "I make no attempt to steer the boat; all my energies are directed toward keeping it afloat." *Ceteris paribus,* the situation seems not dissimilar in the Roman Catholic Church today. The writer of this article does not know whether it would be wise to put into practice all his suggestions at once; he knows that it would be courageous. He writes frankly and trenchantly, to serve the cause of truth. If anything seems offensive, he begs forgiveness for ignorance or insensitivity. He offers his proposals in a spirit of modesty and humility.

*Humanae Vitae* has caused a grave setback to ecumenical relations between the Roman Catholic Church and other Churches. Little has been pronounced publicly, but much has been said privately. Although non-Romans have been brought closer to their Roman fellow-Christians in brotherly sympathy, they have been dismayed at what has happened. Firstly, most Churches hold that the pope's teaching on contraception is erroneous, while some of their members would regard it as pernicious. Second, the apparent disregard by the pope of the advice

117

of a majority of qualified theologians and laymen on the commission which he himself appointed, and his authoritative exposition of natural law as though it were an aspect of revealed law, has increased their dismay. Third, the failure of the pope to consult the college of bishops on a matter of such importance, so soon after the promulgation of the *Constitution on the Church* at Vatican Council II, has added to their bewilderment. Finally, the divergence of views on the nature of authority, resulting from the conflicting claims of private conscience and ecclesiastical obedience, has led to a confused state of affairs within the Roman Catholic Church herself and needs further clarification.

There are several courageous things that the pope could do to reestablish ecumenical confidence, and to complete the *aggiornamento* which Pope John XXIII inaugurated:

1. According to Vatican Council I, when the Roman pontiff defines a doctrine of faith or morals *ex cathedra,* "such a definition of itself and not by virtue of the consent of the Church is irreformable". Thus the pope need never consult the college of bishops at all. According to Vatican Council II, "the episcopal order is the subject of supreme and full power over the universal Church, together with her head, the Roman pontiff, and never without this head". After the publication of *Humanae Vitae,* safeguards have become necessary to ensure that the Church manifests her true nature. It would be courageous for the pope to declare, on his own and not by the consent of the Church, that in future all papal pronouncements of major importance will have the prior agreement of the college of bishops. Such courageous action would greatly restore ecumenical confidence, although it must be admitted that even such consultation comes far short of synodical government as understood in the Church of England, for it does not do justice to the role of priests and laymen in making such decisions.

2. It is evident to anyone reading *Humanae Vitae* that a chief preoccupation is to retain and safeguard the past traditional teaching of the Roman Church on contraception. It would be courageous for the pope to declare that despite the manifold

guidance of the Holy Spirit in the past, the Church of Rome has on occasions erred, and that God has on occasions given guidance to other Churches from which the Roman Church could profit. Such a declaration would not involve any insuperable theological problems. Far from detracting from the authority of the Roman Catholic Church today, it would actually add to it. Doctrine must take account of what has actually happened—and everyone knows that the Church was wrong about Galileo, and that she changed her mind about usury. A generous admission of past error and a recognition of the Holy Spirit's guidance outside the Roman Catholic Church would show great courage, honesty and humility, and it would evoke a loving and sympathetic response outside the Roman Church as well as within her.

3. The jurisdiction of the pope was defined at Vatican Council I in absolutist terms. Before *Humanae Vitae* it seemed that people would come to trust the pope never to use his universal jurisdiction absolutely. However, after *Humanae Vitae,* with its claims even on secular governments, it is hopeless to expect this confidence to develop, nor would it be soundly based if it did. What is needed is "an evangelical renunciation of spiritual power" (H. Küng, *The Church,* Burns & Oates, London 1967, p. 472). If the present pope were to make such a declaration now, future popes could make it on their acceptance of the papal office immediately after their election. If the principle of subsidiarity is to have its full force, the time is propitious for a practical delimitation of power in the various spheres of the pope's activity. For example, the pope's exercise of jurisdiction as a diocesan or provincial is very different from that of primate of the Roman Catholic Church or of chief pastor of the universal Church.

4. In the absence of an ecumenical council, the pope is the only organ, according to Roman Catholic belief, whereby infallible pronouncements can be made. At the same time it is becoming increasingly clear that past definitions are inadequate for present problems. It would be an act of great courage if the pope were to declare *ex cathedra* that past definitions are no longer binding in new situations where questions must be asked again in

the light of new knowledge and in fresh contexts, and that all definitions by their nature can give only "an imperfect, incomplete, unclear, partial and fragmentary" delineation of the mysteries of truth (cf. H. Küng, *op. cit.*, p. 343). Such a declaration would not only greatly help ecumenical relations but would meet the desire for *aggiornamento* within the Roman Church herself.

5. Everywhere today there seems a crisis of authority. It is seen in family life. It is found in schools and universities. In politics it is seen in Communist countries as much as in Western democracies or neutral administrations. The pope would put all Christendom in his debt if he were to take the courageous step of setting up a mixed commission (including non-Roman Catholic observers and consultants) to report to him on the relation between ecclesiastical obedience and private conscience, and to publicly declare their findings.

6. Every Church must have ecclesiastical administration. However flexible and decentralized government may be, there is bound to be central authority and central administration, and the pope needs theological and ecclesiastical advisers. Non-Roman Christians, for the most part, know little about the Roman Curia, but it would seem that, even after Vatican Council II, its influence is excessive. The suspicion is even voiced that the pope's own freedom of action and decision is under some constraint because of its power. Curial administrators seem predominantly Italian by race and conservative in attitude. If the Roman Catholic Church is to vindicate her catholicity in the eyes of non-Roman Christians as well as her own members, it must be plain to see that the Roman Curia is fully internationalized and clearly subordinate to the college of bishops of which the pope is the head.

7. Many non-Roman Christians feel that the pope, by reason of the present structure of his office, is too remote from ordinary life to be universally regarded as the vicar of Christ. In marked contrast to Christ himself during his public ministry, the pope, despite his foreign visits and his strenuous efforts at home, is surrounded by the paraphernalia of power and by the de-

humanizing routines of official administration. It is not enough for the pope's life to be marked by profound religious observance and devout personal piety. If he is to be recognized by all Christians as their chief pastor and spiritual leader, he must share to a far greater extent the ordinary life and the ordinary pleasures, duties and temptations of ordinary men. How can this be done? It would be a courageous act that would win the sympathy of all Christendom (and non-Christians as well) if the pope were to spend a period in a different diocese (and in a different country) each year, living with the diocesan bishop and sharing his *episcope,* meeting not merely the clergy but also the laity in their everyday affairs. No doubt this would cause difficult problems of publicity and administration, but they would not be insuperable. There would be diplomatic problems too, but the voluntary renunciation of power that the pope would already have made would presumably include renunciation of his diplomatic status as head of State. Somehow the pope must be seen to be *servus servorum Dei.* He must share, and be seen to share, in the ordinary life of men. Such an act of self-abnegation and humility, after the pattern of Christ, would warm and win the hearts of men, and give a practical outlet for the expression of charity and for the exercise of a pastoral ministry. This leads to a further suggestion. The pope's increasing share in the ordinary ways of life should not exclude the possibility of a voluntary retirement from office, a supreme act of papal humility and self-abnegation. At a time when the speed of change in the world resembles an exponential curve, old age may be seen as an impediment rather than as an asset in the exercise of the chief pastoral office in the Church.

8. The pope would give practical expression to his leadership in the college of bishops if he were to take the courageous action of calling another ecumenical council to affirm and ratify these other acts of courage which he would have previously carried out.

These suggestions are all made in the hope that they may bring forward the day for which so many hope and pray, when autonomous and autochthonous Churches may be united not merely in increasing love and sympathy and understanding, but also in communion with one another under the presidency of the bishop of Rome.

---

## A PROTESTANT VIEWPOINT
Hendrikus Berkhof, Leiden, Netherlands

Many may think this a rather abstract question in the present situation. Nobody will deny that the present pope has courage. In some cases this courage has worked in favor of ecumenical understanding; in many others it has hampered it. When we look at it from an evangelical and Dutch angle, the overall result is negative. By far the greater number of non-Catholic Christians will hardly blame the present pope for that, but rather see it as inherent in the papal office as such. It is this office which is considered the greatest obstacle to ecumenical understanding. One can only think of one courageous action the occupant of the Holy See could take to help ecumenism, and his action happens to be totally unthinkable: by a last act of the exercise of his infallibility he could revoke this infallibility and abolish it. And so the "pope" and "ecumenical understanding" seem to exclude each other.

Yet, if I see the situation correctly, there seems to be a small but growing group of evangelical theologians and believers who dare expose themselves, although as yet purely theoretically, to thinking about a possible ecumenical part which the papacy could play. This adventurous thought is no doubt the echo of the courageous biblical reassessment of the "Petrine office" undertaken by various groups of Catholic theologians. This reassessment does not seek to introduce any new elements but merely to lay bare the basic biblical structure of this Petrine office. This is at present the most important ecumenical step taken with regard to the papal office. And it is of decisive importance precisely because the unification of the Church can only take place on the ground of a common understanding of what the Bible proclaims.

But this is not the question asked in the heading of this article: What can the pope do himself? One can hardly expect him to throw open a discussion about the continuity of his office with that formerly exercized by Peter. But this is as much an advantage as a disadvantage. Officially he believes that his office has existed since the New Testament and that it is identical with that of Peter at that time. One has but to think of the three texts in the dome of St. Peter's. Therefore, one may expect of him that it is of primary importance for him to take the new examination of the role of St. Peter seriously, since this study aims at understanding the relevant texts in their various contexts with the help of form-criticism and the study of the composition of the documents as has been done recently in Catholic theology by authors like Hans Küng (*The Church*) and Patrick Dias (*Vielfalt der Kirche in der Vielfalt der Jünger, Zeugen und Diener*). This should be the easier for the pope as this new research indeed shows the variety of traditions about Peter but makes it also clear that Peter's authority rests on a very old and common tradition. The obvious clarity of this tradition points to a close connection with the message of salvation.

The question about this connection might be formulated as follows: Why precisely was Simon Bar-jona chosen to be the rock of the Church? The answer as given in the New Testament, at least in my view and accepted by a growing number of Catholic exegetes, is because, through his peculiar history of loyalty and betrayal, of defection and forgiveness, Peter became the outstanding example of what life means in Christ's Church. It is a life based on forgiveness of sins and overcoming scandal. It is Peter who, representing all the others, promises Jesus to be faithful, opposes Jesus' passion, denies the Lord, receives the message of the resurrection, is accepted in grace and is given a leading function in the Church. He, who representatively denied Christ, can, for that very reason, become the representative of Christ. It is

Peter, brought lower than the others, who knows what it means to live by grace alone in the justification of the sinner.

Immediately connected with this is the unique kind of authority of Peter. His denial and his authority are complementary to each other. He has authority because he knows better than anyone else what grace means. As the humblest of all he can be the leader of all. If one wanted to introduce here the concept of "infallibility", one could say that Peter could not fail in his guidance because he knew how badly he had failed himself and for that reason stood wholly open to the function of helping and correcting the brethren (as Gal. 1, 7-14 shows). As Patrick Dias put it: "The Church is the community as freed by Jesus from the tyranny of sin and so living in the hope of her final deliverance and redemption. For that reason she neither can nor may underrate or ignore the constant threat of eschatological defection, the dark reality of her life. Peter, himself the stumbling block and rock of the Church, is witness to and evidence of this real danger of sin and defection, and has as such a basic significance for the Church of all ages. He therefore has a function which must constantly be filled in and for the Church. As saved from sin, constantly dependent on grace and its invincible power, enlightened by the revelation of the Father and in this light professing Jesus as the Christ, in short, as he who is constantly carried by the Lord, Peter is the rocklike foundation of the Church." [1]

For me the main ecumenical question with regard to the Petrine office is this: Is the officeholder capable of existentially embodying in himself the unique and at the same time exemplary dialectic of this function? In this case indeed, Christ's promise will be wholly fulfilled: "And once you have been converted, you in your turn must strengthen your brethren" (Lk. 22, 32). As long as a pope puts himself above his brethren by stressing his authority (even with the best of intentions), he runs the risk of breaking his solidarity with them in their temptations by his dogmatizing or moralizing and so will discourage them instead of

---

[1] P. Dias, *Vielfalt der Kirche in der Vielfalt der Jünger, Zeugen und Diener* (Freiburg/Basel/Wien, 1968), p. 195.

strengthening them. The pope's own subjection to temptation and fallibility in the right exercise of the Petrine office is not a concession but a confession.

If the pope could see his function of strengthening in this light, it would soon be clear that the circle of brethren strengthened by him extends far beyond that of his fellow-bishops. His office would then become an ecumenical function, for the People of God throughout the world understand essentially everywhere the same temptations. The fact that someone has a worldwide office, and therefore sees more than others, could meet a genuine need of Christ's community, particularly in our time. Everything, therefore, depends on how the one who holds this office conceives of his relation to the brethren, and puts it into practice.

Does this imply a courageous gesture on the part of the pope? He must do something that is so essential to Christian existence as such that the word "courageous" is hardly the right one. I hope I may be forgiven if I express this in a very sharp and very "Protestant" way: he must die as pope in order to rise again as Peter. In other words, he must lose his *auctoritas* and *potestas* (authority and power) in order to win them.

*Auctoritas* is a category of encounter. One has it or one does not. Whether or not someone has it cannot be determined by that person himself; it can only be established by those for the sake of whom he wishes to be committed with his "authority". One who has to constantly refer to his authority, nervously or threateningly, does not have genuine authority, but only he who forgets himself and his authority in order to serve the brethren (Luke), the sheep (John), the "little ones" (who form the context in the passage about the power of the keys in Matthew 18). Only those should speak of his authority who are strengthened by him in their faith and therefore can thank God for this person and his office.

In concrete terms, this means that the pope really ceases to worry about his authority and only cares for one thing: to strengthen, to encourage, to console and to exhort the People of God in the broadest sense on their pilgrimage. He will then not have to be afraid to say something hard and unpopular; precisely because he will not put it on their shoulders as an external burden but rather as a brotherly question put to the Christian conscience, he will find the whole world listening. Nor will he be afraid to revoke statements made by himself or his predecessors. Such a fear is typical of political or industrial "bosses", and their claim to infallibility is rightly seen as a proof of their fallibility. Only a man who is free in the deepest sense can afford to revoke a decision. A successor of Peter who recognizes that he can err and who "puts his trust in nothing but the grace that will be given" (cf. 1 Pet. 1, 13) will become credible to the whole *oecumene* (the whole Christian household) and beyond as the bearer of genuine authority.

The time will soon come when the Churches in the secularized world will have to pull together in such a way that the question of a common leadership will become urgent. We shall then have to look for a "president of the community of love". Ignatius of Antioch had no doubt that he could find him in Rome. Could that happen to us again?

---

## AN ORTHODOX VIEWPOINT
Basil Exarchos, Thessalonica, Greece

I shall try to answer this question in fairly general terms, leaving it up to the pope and the Catholic Church to decide upon a course of implementation.

As the ecumenical patriarch of Constantinople, Athenagoras I, has pointed out repeatedly, we have moved away from each other and created divisions in the sphere of practical action; therefore we must meet each other and reunite in the sphere of practical action. Our practical actions must be suffused with the love of Christ, which St. Paul described in detail (1 Cor. 13, 4f.).

Patriarch Athenagoras has also noted that the task of the

Church scholar [1]—i.e., the theologian—is to investigate theoretical problems and make his findings available to the Church's
leadership. Therefore, we theologians, as possessors of this particular charism in the Church community, should offer our services to this basic desire of the Church. Here I should like to single
out several points, related to the initiatives of Vatican Council II,
which I feel could foster ecumenical understanding between the
Orthodox Church and the Catholic Church.

1. In the Eastern Church, there is a stronger appreciation of
the Church as a community; [2] in the West, the Church as an
institution dominates people's experience and activity.

In Christian antiquity, the principle of the Spirit and his tradition was the determining factor in the Church. After the time of
Alexander the Great, the spiritual centers maintained their importance despite the new political changes, for they remained
more or less intimately associated with the spiritual, intellectual
and social elements of life. In that era, the *pentarchia* became the
constitutional and governmental framework of the first Christian
*ecumene*. While rivalry did crop up, particularly when new political formations were attempted, the basic system continued to
survive intact.

With the coming of new times and a new Christian *ecumene*,
efforts to maintain the old tradition came to seem one-sided and
biased. From this period derive many forms which no longer can
prove satisfactory to the "mature world" of the second *ecumene*.
We speak of a "new age" or of "different times". We should like
to view the situation in Christian and ecclesial terms, envisioning
a "higher" stage of development to be reached by the second
*ecumene*. In this context we must point out that Christendom as a
whole should pay closer attention to the "signs of the times" and
make a greater effort to interpret them correctly.

2. It is commonly asserted that the Catholic Church represents
the institutional thrust (in her monarchical form specifically),

---

[1] See also my comments in "Die gegenwärtige wissenschaftliche und
kirchliche Verantwortung der Theologie," in *Kyrios* (1964), pp. 262-76.
[2] See my article, "Das soziale Problem als ein innerkirchliches Problem," in *Festschrift für Prof. Dr. D. Alivisatos* (1958), pp. 579-92.

while the Orthodox Church is committed to the communal
and "democratic" principle. Now the fact is that the institutional and monarchical element also has its legitimate place in
the Orthodox Church, even if only on the episcopal level, and the
democratic principle applies, more or less, to the relationship
between bishops themselves. Yet, it is true enough that the notion of centralized government did predominate in the Catholic
Church.

In recent times, however, there has been a shift in this tendency also. Vatican Council II has indeed inaugurated a new
epoch in the Catholic Church. What this will mean for the future
of the Church is something we cannot say exactly right now. But
I should like to suggest some lines of governmental development
that would accord with Orthodox sentiments about the Church.

Decentralization of Catholic Church government should be
gradually carried out in the near future. Restructuring and fuller
coordination should take place on every level. Vertical ties will be
shored up by horizontal relationships, which will give full play to
the principle of collective responsibility and collective control
without jeopardizing the vertical ties.

Since Vatican Council II, attempts are being made to build
dioceses from the community level up. Now efforts must be made
to build the whole Church from the diocesan level up, creating a
whole series of multi-leveled but organically related units, from
the local eucharistic community to the highest worldwide unit of
government. In the sphere of secular government, too, our century has seen the rise of worldwide organizations, like the League
of Nations and the United Nations. Christendom and the Church
dare not run the risk of remaining provincial.

Such a development in the Catholic Church would also benefit
the Orthodox Church. It would make us conscious of our narrow
sectarianism, and compel us to profess unity to our fellow-
Christians and non-Christians in our daily life and activities.
Obviously, this will greatly help to promote and facilitate the
process of dialogue. In the life of the Church herself, it will help
us to sense which way the wind is blowing, and how we should

actively participate in the development of the second *ecumene* in accordance with the Lord's command.

3. Another tendency must be reexamined: the effort to distinguish the charisms (i.e., vocations and ministries) associated with the altar from those that are to be exercised outside the altar. The attempt to draw an absolutely clear line between these two types of charisms must be abandoned. In short, we must face up to the problem of the "laity".

Lay people are full-fledged members of the Church community. Thus they are entitled to exercise functions pertaining to the life of the Church. All of us know that the ministry of the altar represents a special function. But we must also realize that other functions (i.e., charisms) of the utmost spiritual importance may be exercised without any tieup to the altar.

The charism of doctrinal teaching and scholarly research into the spiritual life of the Church is an eminent function, but there is no reason why it has to be associated with the altar. The Orthodox Church, for example, has always had *lay theologians;* only since Vatican Council II has the Catholic Church begun to move in that direction.

4. Mutual enrichment between the Christian East and the Christian West ceased completely with the schism of the 11th century. Now this mutual enrichment could take place once again, with both sides *adopting useful ideas and forms* from the original Christian *ecumene*.

This process of adoption, unfortunately, would not be easy to accomplish. Right now the Orthodox Church herself is not in a position[3] to offer updated material. This means that the West must take the initiative in rescuing the treasures of the original *ecumene* from the underground vaults of history. Obviously, such an effort will benefit the East as well, which finds itself in an oppressive situation at the present time. In this way we can make authentic dialogue possible and contribute to some real results.

Through study of, and familiarity with, the ecumenical tradition, scholars will be able to conduct a dialogue that is objective

[3] See my article, "Theologische Probleme der modernen Orthodoxie," in *Theologia* (Athens, 1965), pp. 255-69.

and as comprehensive as possible. If it is to be truly comprehensive, it must be conducted between scholars who share a common store of knowledge. The study of Eastern tradition must also be given new vitality in Eastern circles.

The study of Eastern tradition by Western scholars, of itself, will not lead to a common understanding in East-West dialogue. For the representatives of the Eastern Church would not be familiar with the experiences and teachings of the Western Church that date from the inception of the second Christian *ecumene*. If we are seriously interested in dialogue, we must see to it that the Eastern participants get appropriate information about the Western tradition.

Needless to say, the number of dialogue participants must be relatively proportional on both sides, if the dialogue is to be conducted on the proper level. If these conditions are not met satisfactorily, great difficulties will be encountered. The Western Church enjoys a large measure of freedom in her living situation; only small areas are closed off. Moreover, she has a large number of scholars at her disposal. Thus she could do much more to promote a meaningful and up-to-date dialogue.

5. It seems to me that dialogue in the course of everyday living is just as important as dialogue on the scholarly level. What exactly do I mean?

Well, we all should realize that the experience we gain in daily human intercourse does away with many misunderstandings and helps to bring human beings together. Now we must strive to accomplish the same thing in our Christian life, both within and outside the precincts of the Church. Religious ceremonies, prayers and cultic worship must be made accessible to Christians of both Churches; their Christian meaning and their actual execution must not be kept from the people. If the faithful have access to these things, they will learn to distinguish religious essentials from accidentals.

How these things will shape up concretely is something I prefer not to discuss here. I am content to have called attention to a few points.

# PART III
## DOCUMENTATION
## CONCILIUM

**Office** of the Executive Secretary
*Nijmegen, Netherlands*

Concilium General Secretariat/*Nijmegen, Netherlands*

# Ecumenical Experiments

## INTRODUCTION

When an international review of theology publishes a volume on ecumenical experiments, it owes it to itself to give a bird's-eye view of what concrete results have been achieved in ecumenism at the international level. We have tried to do this by asking experts to report on their findings in the various cultural regions: in East and West, in young Churches and Churches that seem to have become set in a rocklike institutionalization, in communities that are growing toward each other under a Marxist regime, and in Churches that try to steer their own course under a capitalist constellation.

In seeking contributions to this section, we emphasized that we were not looking for the expression of ecumenical wishes but rather for an objective report on actual results. The survey will show that ecumenism is not merely the "talk" of ironical ecclesiastical "society", but also an evangelical leaven that pervades the dough of Christendom in order to become a bread which can be true nourishment for modern man, already dreaming of one world. The separatist mentality has disappeared and the new mentality has begun to express itself in visible results. There is still much to do, but much has already been achieved. We must also have the courage to accept these positive results consciously; otherwise we would lose the courage to continue with what must still be done.

---

ECUMENICAL EXPERIMENTS IN NORTH AMERICA
David Bowman, S.J., Bronx, New York

This large continent is far different from any other in the extent and variety of ecumenical activities. One apology should be made, among the many that will seem necessary: Mexico and French-speaking Canada are not included in the survey. Fathers Irenée Beaubien and Stefan Valquette have done great things in and from their ecumenical center in Montreal; the Canadian French are omitted here not because they are doing little, but rather because they are doing much—too much to be included in detail in such a sketchy outline.

The Bishops' Committee for Ecumenical and Interreligious Affairs in Washington, D.C. is staffed by Fathers Bernard Law and John Hotchkin. The committee is composed of fourteen bishop-members, selected by the National Conference of Catholic Bishops. They supervise all official dialogues with other Christian denominations. Subcommittees are approved for the following bilateral discussions: with the National Council of Churches, the American Baptist Church, the Disciples of Christ, the Episcopal Church, the Lutheran Church in America, the Methodist Church, the Orthodox Church and the Presbyterian-Reformed Alliance. Topics discussed have been varied, such as mixed marriages, eucharistic sharing, religious liberty, teaching authority in the Church and government aid to Church-related schools. Interreligious dialogue with the Jews goes on apace under the direction of Father Edward Flannery, whose office is at Seton Hall University.

In Canada, the director of the English secretariat of the National Commission on Ecumenism is Father John Keating. Here there are no formal bilateral groups, but Roman Catholic observer-delegates sit at the Anglican-United Church negotiations, and they attend the General Assembly of the United Church of Canada and the Anglican Committee on Roman

Catholic Relations. A Lutheran-Roman Catholic dialogue is developing, and extensive interreligious activity is under way with the Jews.

An annual workshop in ecumenism has been run for five years by diocesan ecumenical officers and is becoming a major factor in American ecumenism. Held in Detroit in June, 1968, its speakers included Eugene Carson Blake, Archbishop John Deardon, Godfrey Diekmann and Joseph Gremillion.

In the National Council of Churches, all divisions are becoming more ecumenical. In 1968, the Medical Mission Sisters joined the Division of Overseas Ministry, and the Confraternity of Christian Doctrine entered an agreement with the Division of Christian Education to work together on curricular materials and teacher-training. The main thrust is through the Division of Christian Unity under the leadership of Mrs. Theodore Wedel. A Joint Working Group, under the co-chairmanship of Archbishop Carberry and the Reverend John Coventry Smith, has met twice annually since 1966, with such encouraging results that a small committee is now working on preliminaries to a formal discussion of full membership of the Roman Catholic Church in some ecumenical cooperative, to be worked out. Canada, too, has a Joint Working Group, formed in 1968.

The major theological effort of the Department of Faith and Order has been the annual colloquium, bringing together 100 scholars from almost all theological traditions of the United States. The subjects discussed have been conversion, evangelization, and the notion of salvation. In Canada, special studies have been conducted by the English secretariat on mixed marriages, baptism and non-believers.

Faith and Order has also cooperated on two ecumenical conferences on Christian worship, where attendance has included about 200 Lutherans, Episcopalians and Roman Catholics.

Ecumenical publications include *Unity Trends,* a bi-monthly publication which provides news, documentation, interviews and reviews of ecumenical import. Also significant are *The Lamp, The Ecumenist* and *The Journal of Ecumenical Studies. The Re-*

*vised Standard Version* of Scripture appeared in 1952, with a Catholic edition in 1966.

*Living Room Dialogues,* a study-action book in two volumes, has been used by about 8,000 couples from differing Christian traditions. It frequently serves as a carryover from the Week of Prayer for Christian Unity.

Special mention must be made of this latter ecumenical project, for it is the best "grass-roots" ecumenism that we have, and is practically the only event reaching all dioceses. The Week of Prayer leaflet has the mutual support of the World and National Councils of Churches and is recommended by the Bishops' Committee for Ecumenical and Interreligious Affairs. The week is usually celebrated with services held each evening in various churches of a neighborhood. Frequently this unity in prayer has led to common Bible-study groups and social-action projects. Reformation Day services are now usually "Festivals of Faith" celebrating a common renewal in the Church.

Locally, there exist, in almost every state in America, local councils of Churches, and in about forty geographic areas Roman Catholic dioceses or parishes are full members of the state or metropolitan Council of Churches. In Texas, the ten Roman Catholic dioceses have joined the former Texas Council of Churches to form the Texas Conference of Churches—a new ecumenical form in this country. In Canada, regional meetings of diocesan officers have produced common guidelines on ecumenism.

The Consultation of Church Union has met since 1962 with ten national Churches in dialogue. The Association of American Theological Schools now includes some Catholic seminaries. The Gustave Weigel Society promotes spiritual ecumenism. There are increasing numbers of centers like Bergamo in Dayton, Ohio, the Graymoor Ecumenical Institute in Garrison, New York, and St. John's Abbey Ecumenical Institute of Research in Collegeville, Minnesota. The University Christian Movement in 1966 coalesced major Protestant student groups and two Roman Catholic college organizations.

Social programs have developed in the areas of peace, the Spanish-speaking and migrant ministries, and the Delta ministry in Mississippi. Catholic Relief Service works closely with Church World Service on overseas ministry. Cooperative Church ministry is taking new forms in the "New City" of Columbia, Maryland, and in St. Mark's Parish in Kansas City, Missouri, where four pastors from four traditions service an inner city community, sharing all in common except the eucharist. The Urban Training Center in Chicago is an ecumenical program of training for ministry to inner city peoples.

Next to Pope John, Cardinal Bea embodied ecumenism for us. His visits to America delighted and enriched us. May his spirit, and that of Fathers John Courtney Murray and Gustave Weigel impel us on the path they trod so kindly, toward complete unity in Christ.

---

ECUMENICAL EXPERIMENTS IN ENGLAND
Robert Jeffery, London, England

The term "ecumenical experiment" has come to be used in a special sense as a result of the Faith and Order Conference of the British Council of Churches held at Nottingham in 1964. That conference asked the Churches to "designate areas of ecumenical experiment, at the request of local congregations or in new towns and housing areas. In such areas there should be experiments in ecumenical group ministries, in sharing buildings and equipment and in the development of mission" (*Unity Begins at Home*, S.C.M. Press 1964, p. 79).

In the previous twenty years there had been a rapid growth in Britain of local councils of Churches, where Christians met together and shared in some common activities such as services of public witness, youth work and joint Church papers. The

Nottingham resolution has set on foot a growing development of much closer cooperation, usually under the name of an "ecumenical experiment". This cooperation normally takes the form of a building shared by various Churches and is often linked with some form of shared ministry. One of the earliest of these to be established was at Blackbird Leys, a housing estate near Oxford, where an Anglican church is shared with members of the Free Churches. There are two clergymen; one is an Anglican; the other is a Congregationalist who is paid and supported by the Methodist, Presbyterian, Baptist, Congregational and Society of Friends congregations in Oxford, and he acts on behalf of them all. The Roman Catholic Church is also on the same site as the church, and both are next door to the community center through which the clergy wish to serve and keep in contact with the residents of the housing estate. The pattern of worship is of separate sacramental worship, but there is a joint service in the evenings. This is the kind of pattern which is now developing widely throughout Britain. A recent survey of this (see R. Jeffery, *Areas of Ecumenical Experiment,* B.C.C. 1968) has revealed that there are some 200 presently in existence or in advanced stage of planning. Many of these are in new towns and housing estates.

The problems of establishing such "areas of ecumenical experiment" are very considerable. There has been a large number of legal problems which it is hoped will be overcome by a new bill which is being presented to Parliament. This will enable church buildings to be shared on an equal basis by two or more denominations. There are also difficult financial problems because the salary scale for clergy varies between the Churches, and also the amount of support required from the local Churches by the denominations varies considerably.

The main point of tension in such an "ecumenical experiment" inevitably arises over the eucharist. When congregations live and work together, they often reach the point of wishing to share in the eucharist together. In some Churches the congregations continue to have separate eucharists; in others, various means have been devised to surmount the problem. A few Churches have adopted a pattern of parallel celebration whereby two clergy celebrate the eucharist with separate elements for their own people at the same service, using one rite. Another pattern is for clergy of different denominations to "concelebrate" at one eucharist. Both patterns are open to theological criticism, but both do enable the congregations to come together in eucharistic worship.

Such attempts at sharing usually involve cooperation with any children and young people, though when they reach the age of admission to full membership they are usually taught denominationally.

Other forms of joint activity include various forms of service to the local community (looking after old people, care of the sick, hospital visiting, etc.), and sometimes the running of a Bible Week. In a Bible Week, Churches of many traditions join together for exposition and study of a chosen theme from Scripture. This can be a very useful way of deepening each other's faith and understanding each other.

As part of the follow-up of the Nottingham Conference, in conjunction with the Conference of British Missionary Societies, the British Council of Churches launched a major study program entitled "The People Next Door". This was the largest experiment in ecumenical lay education which has ever taken place in Britain, and some 90,000 people took part. The program lasted six weeks, during which Christians of all denominations met together in small groups in houses to consider how they could help to fulfill the mission of God in their locality and throughout the world. The findings of these groups provide a very useful analysis of the current ecclesiastical scene in Britain (see C. Sansbury *et al., Agenda for the Churches*, S.C.M. 1967). The effects of the program in initiating further ecumenical action and experiment will continue for some considerable time. It is made clear in these findings that much can happen, provided there is a willingness for it. "Ecumenical experiments", in terms of joint ministry and mission, could become normative in Britain if only that willingness will grow. One group which took part in "The People Next Door" program put it like this: "Here, where ecumenical relations have been very good for a long time, it is going to be difficult to take the next step toward unity, for this time we must be ready to abandon some of our independence." The fostering of such willingness is the main ecumenical task in Britain today.

---

ECUMENICAL EXPERIMENTS IN THE BRITISH ISLES
John Coventry, S.J., Heythrop, England

It is not possible to write about ecumenical development in the British Isles, which includes four countries and three hierarchies all moving at different paces. In England the chief partner in dialogue is the Church of England, in Wales the Free Churches, in Scotland the Presbyterian Church of Scotland. In Ireland, where Church relations are inextricably mixed with politics, one sees no reason why the Catholics should ever join a British Council of Churches, to which the other Irish Churches belong, or why the latter should ever be submerged beneath the Catholics in an Irish Council of Churches. In Ireland one must say that, in spite of the heroic efforts of small groups, ecumenism has not yet touched bishops, priests and people on the Catholic side. In Scotland a considerable ecumenical movement is under way, but it has gained less acceptance among Christians generally than in England and Wales, and so the ensuing remarks will limit themselves to these latter territories.

Owing to the tendency of the hierarchy to await instructions from above, rather than to take or allow initiatives, there was a slow start, but ecumenism is now developing fairly rapidly among Catholics. There is a complex and variegated ecclesial scene, apart from the complexities of Anglicanism itself, in a country where a number of Protestant bodies, including the Quakers and the Salvation Army, originated historically and have different social or territorial allegiances. Such flexibility assists the movement, which is always capable of development in some direction, and is not likely to reach a stalemate, or "ecumenical fatigue", too easily.

The British are an empirical people. They are not theorists, and pay scant attention or respect to what "the experts" are saying or doing. Hence their real ecumenical interest and experience today is not concerned with such matters as joint Bible translation (which is an international affair, and for experts), though the Revised Standard Version is becoming the most common text, or with other religions as such, though social relations with Hindus and Pakistanis are a pressing problem, and though small elite groups are concerned with Judaism, nor with intercommunion, which is not very much desired as yet by or with Catholics. Rather, the immediate and vivid experience is simply that of getting to know religiously their ordinary neighbors, with whom the rest of life has long been shared. It is felt to be of supreme importance that ecumenism should involve everyone, and not be a matter for clergy and enthusiasts only, and that it should be measured by developments at village level, rather than by isolated events that hit the headlines. The pace may be slower, but the transformation is more solid. In all this, there are everywhere to be found groups of laity that are ahead of most of their priests, and groups of priests who are ahead of their bishops.

At the national level, formal relationships and conversations are rapidly growing: with Anglicans, with Methodists, with Evangelicals, and with the Free Churches in Wales. There is growing participation in the British Council of Churches: a BCC/RC Joint Working Group has just produced its first report, accepted by both sponsoring bodies; a Catholic priest has become a staff member of the BCC; there is an increasing Catholic share in all national ecumenical conferences.

At the local level, more and more local councils of Churches are admitting Catholics as full members, and it is felt that this partnership must grow, and mutual trust must be widely built up, before the Catholic Church can appropriately become a member of the British Council of Churches. Local growth depends almost entirely on the extent to which a diocese has promoted (or even set up) a diocesan ecumenical commission, and so there are "backward" and "forward" dioceses. Conferences are beginning to be organized for boys and girls at different schools of a given area, as a promotion of ecumenism among Christian youth—who in Britain are conservative rather than radical. Similar conferences for teachers are thought to be the best means of promoting ecumenical education, rather than centers or books; ecumenical teaching is not a matter of syllabus, but of how you teach. There is growing cooperation everywhere in the tackling of social problems. "The People Next Door" campaign, organized by the Church of England, was the kind of thing that had special appeal to the British empirical temperament, and Catholics joined it widely. House groups for ecumenical prayer and discussion are growing everywhere. In general, a widespread process of ecumenical education is spreading.

Yet there are very pressing needs, and one has to record that some basic ecumenical problems have hardly begun to find their solution. Many priests have accepted invitations to preach in other pulpits, mainly Anglican, without being ready to return the invitation. Steps toward mutual recognition of baptism are slow, but there is hope of an agreement being reached through the British Council of Churches. Mixed marriages are the chief obstacle in the eyes of other Christians, yet few of our bishops and priests have yet seized the implication of the Instruction of March, 1966, let alone pressed forward: a stalemate has ensued, with the bishops awaiting further instructions from Rome, and Rome apparently awaiting the formation of a policy by local hierarchies. One can quote a single instance of Catholics and Anglicans planning to build a common church in a new town, but clergy and people in general, apart from the universities, have barely begun to think in terms of shared premises of any kind. One can quote a team ministry at a London airport using a common chapel, but bishops and priests in general have not begun to think of the opportunities of ecumenical team ministries. In Britain, these things will grow from the bottom by experiment, rather than be planned and implemented from above.

---

## ECUMENICAL EXPERIMENTS IN LATIN AMERICA
Jorge Mejía, Buenos Aires, Argentina

Until a short time ago, the South American continent would have struck the observer as impervious to ecumenical activity. However, there were some signs that the post-conciliar years would bring a change. The present writer has described in a short article the factors with which the dawning ecumenical initiatives would have to contend. The religious tradition of this continent is Hispanic, post-Tridentine, regalist—even in its more liberal tendencies—and, in practice if not in theory, opposed to the idea of religious freedom. This was the Catholic picture; the Evangelical side presented a similar one.

The above-mentioned article appeared in the November-December 1963 issue of *The Ecumenist*. Since then the situation has changed considerably, or it is at least on the way to considerable changes. If the negative factors have not disappeared, they have at least become fossilized, and, most important of all they are much more readily seen to be negative. There is also the possibility of joint initiatives to overcome them, while those who are interested in maintaining the previous state of affairs are obliged to take a defensive attitude—and to justify it.

The question of the Evangelical missions in Latin America, which is linked to the question of the so-called "sects", though it is wider than this, is obviously a vital field, in which proof of ecumenism in these parts must be given (cf. my article in Volume 14 of *Concilium*). It must be said that the recent emphasis on human advancement and the service of man in general, as values in preparing for evangelization, have not eliminated the difficulty, even if they point to a new way in which it might be solved.

It is precisely in this area of common approach to the human and social reality of Latin America, in tune with the aspirations of the age in which we live, that the greatest progress in coming together, the greatest concentration of effort and the most noteworthy ecumenical achievements can be seen. An indication of this can be observed in the Latin American participation at the "Church and Society" conference held in Geneva in July 1966.

There is, in some cases, a blurring of confessional frontiers. But at the same time it must be recognized that ecumenical movements, with their achievements, do not carry the mass of each religious community with them, nor do they manage to go beyond—at least not always—the divisions among the Churches and Evangelical communities themselves. Latin America has fewer Churches as members of the World Council of Churches than any other region. But a movement has begun and is progressing with the precise aim of uniting all the Evangelical Churches on the continent. Its institutional organ is called the Provisional Commission for Latin American Evangelical Unity (UNELAM). The crisis situation, like that in the European countries under German occupation, or in the concentration camps, favors ecumenical encounter and collaboration. The most ecumenically advanced country in Latin America is possibly Cuba, where the Christian Churches are obliged to look after communities from which all social and official help has been removed, Catholic as well as non-Catholic. Whenever Christian Churches are forced to realize that they are all called to make the Lord present in an increasingly de-Christianized atmosphere, or even a partially Christianized one, their differences come to seem less acute, or at least more worthy of solving. For this to happen, it is essential for the Roman Catholic Church to get rid of the notion that the continent is "Catholic", and for the other Churches to get beyond their negative attitude of recrimination and criticism to a positive attitude of theological dialogue and practical collaboration.

The recent Second General Conference of the Latin American episcopate, held at Medellín in Colombia in August and September 1968, marks a great step forward along this royal road. The observers, representing eleven Christian Churches ranging from the Orthodox (in the person of the Greek Orthodox archbishop of North and South America) to an Evangelist (from UNELAM), saw that the Catholic Church is taking reform "in capite et in membris" seriously, and, without losing her own identity, inviting them to help her in this task, as in others.

Within this general perspective, there is nothing particularly startling about typical ecumenical achievements. The continent already has a New Testament, though not a complete Bible, in common. This was published in Barcelona under the auspices of the monks of Taizé. This fact does serve to underline how desirable it would be to establish a stable and living communication with the fruitful and active Latin American Bible Societies. The day for this is dawning, as some bishops have approved the use by their faithful of the New Testament translation distributed by the Bible Societies—*God Comes to Man* (*Dios llega al hombre*, 1966). Two Catholic observers were invited to the regional assembly of the United Bible Societies at Oaxtepec in Mexico in December 1968.

In the field of mission itself, a difficult one still virtually unexplored by most of our Churches, some attempts at collaboration are beginning. I know of one in the southern part of my own country (Argentina), which was called into being principally by the human needs of those it sets out to evangelize. There are undoubtedly others of which I am unaware. Once this sort of thing is done, other forms of collaboration come to seem entirely normal. The bishops would not oppose them, though they would show some misgivings in case the "sects" took advantage of the changing climate to indulge in proselytizing. By "sects" I mean Jehovah's Witnesses, Seventh Day Adventists and various Evangelical movements whose confessional allegiance is somewhat obscure.

The advanced urban groups, generally drawn together by common social preoccupations, can tend to become virtually autonomous little communities, whose confessional loyalty consequently becomes questionable. They probably practice intercommunion. This is not found in public, however, despite the growing multiplication of common liturgies, some of them at a very official level, like the one held during the Medellín conference. This conference was widely noticed because of the permission sought by and granted to five non-Catholic observers to receive communion at Mass—an Anglican, two Methodists, a Lutheran and a Calvinist. The rest had already left. The permission was granted in response to a petition which included an affirmation of faith in the eucharist, in the light of an interpretation of the Ecumenical Directory of 1967 which at the time still appeared possible. Coldly considered now, the decision seems to have been overhasty, not only because of the repercussions, which were foreseeable and uncontrollable, but because of the lack of adequate preparation for an event of such theological and pastoral importance. But it is also a fact that those present, some 200 bishops, priests and lay people, seem to have received a good impression of the occasion.

In the future, ecumenism in South America should not be disregarded at any level—neither the paradigmatic common or reciprocal gestures, nor the close collaboration in furthering development and promoting human dignity, nor, above all, theological dialogue. But it is important that all these efforts should spring from local initiatives.

## ECUMENICAL EXPERIMENTS IN WEST GERMANY
Johannes Brosseder, Munich, West Germany

As space is limited, certain important aspects of the West German ecumenical scene must be taken on the word of the author—for instance, the fact that ecumenical relations at the parish level are on the whole very satisfactory (e.g., joint study groups and lecture evenings). In both work and worship there is a widespread realization that Christians must cooperate with one another, and this they are now beginning to do with a vigor unique in the history of the Churches. Its basis is the conviction that the furtherance of Jesus' work is a duty they all have in common. It is against this background that the following points must be seen.

Church leaders in the Federal Republic, Austria and Switzerland have established a number of joint commissions and centers whose function is to concern themselves with ecumenical questions and in which members of the different Churches are represented as on equal footing. They are supported in their work by the confessional ecumenical commissions that each Church has established for itself. In addition to these ecclesiastical institutions and commissions, there are also the institutes of ecumenical theology, established at State universities that already have a faculty of theology, which are ecumenically-orientated teaching and research centers.

Up to this time a common celebration of the eucharist has not been possible, although this has not prevented people from worshiping together. Ecumenical liturgies of the Word are commonplace in most areas, and in some places the dialogue sermon—discussion with the congregation—has been found to be very useful in connection with these services. It might also be observed that more could be done with thematically angled services—where, for instance, an event of political significance is made into the theme for a service. One would hope that this practice could be extended and that people might discover other material for these services aside from politics.

With a view to consolidating the practice of common services, a common text of the Our Father has been worked out by Catholics, Protestants and Old Catholics. This is now in use. Work is now being done on a *credo*. Unfortunately the day is still some distance away when we can expect to see a sequence of pericopes prepared for the use of all Christians; the same applies to the hymn book. A new ecumenical Bible translation is being prepared. Agreement on baptismal procedure has been reached between the dioceses and the Church authorities, so that when someone forsakes one Church for another, he is no longer required to be conditionally baptized. To all intents and purposes the Catholic Church now permits conditional baptism only when the Protestant authorities are satisfied that the candidate was not in the first place baptized in accordance with their baptismal rite.

An interconfessional committee responsible for Christian Unity Week prepares texts for the ecumenical services held during this week. This committee comprises representatives of the WCC's Commission on Faith and Order and representatives from Catholic ecumenical centers participating with the approval of the Roman Secretariat for Christian Unity.

At a meeting in Essen (*Katholikentag*), a proper, ecumenical and fully integrated pastoral practice with regard to mixed marriage was demanded, such as the diocese of Passau has had for some while.

In many parts of the country, notably in the diaspora areas, it is already a well-established custom for Catholics and Protestants to use one another's churches for their services. Unhappily, there is still a tendency for each community to build its *own* church, whereas one would have hoped that by now it would be impossible to build a new church without first giving serious thought to the possibility that one church could serve the needs of both communities. Society and Church could benefit considerably if an old people's home or kindergarten were to be built with the money set aside for the church building, if careful examination showed that a second church building was not necessary.

Progress is also being made in the field of education. In most areas Christian community schools are being established instead of perpetuating the old confessional schools. In Bavaria such a school was established as a consequence of popular request, in which the children are educated along Christian lines jointly agreed upon by the relevant Church leaders. For some reason, however, opposition to this procedure was so strong among some of the Catholics concerned that the Bavarian bishops, referring to the Christian basis of the school's educational outlook, commented that they themselves were "still in favor of confessional schools". In spite of this, work is being done on an ecumenical prayer and hymn book for use in the school.

In 1971 there will be an interruption of the annual sequence of Catholic and Protestant Day Conferences in favor of a joint Church Day (*Kirchentag*) which, though it will not amount to a council, will clearly offer strong encouragement to the unity drive within the two Churches.

According to the Ecumenical Institute at Niederaltaich Abbey, which has taken on the job of undertaking practical initiatives in connection with the Reformed Churches, there are now about 200 ecumenical groups in Germany, and among many of them there is very little exchange of contacts or coordination of work. Niederaltaich hopes to be able to improve this situation.

The ecclesiastical academies benefit greatly from the good relationships the Churches have with one another at parish level. For instance, the Protestant centers in Bad Boll and Tutzing work particularly well with their Catholic counterparts in Stuttgart-Hohenheim and Bavaria respectively. One hopes, however, that these centers will make more use of the opportunities that joint study days offer for the development of ecumenical projects. In this way the good will that exists on both sides at parish level could be provided with firmer foundations and clearer objectives. In this respect the ecclesiastical press is playing an invaluable role. The two Protestant weeklies, *Christ und Welt* and *Sonntagsblatt*, and the Catholic weekly, *Publik,* provide comment and documentation that are ecumenically alive and that show a willingness to promote inter-Church collaboration.

The two massive ecclesiastical charitable organizations—the Catholic *Caritas* and the Protestant *Diakonische Hilfswerk*—also undertake joint projects. Their undertakings are often complementary. Much the same can be said of *Misereor* and *Brot für die Welt.* Friday has been jointly proclaimed "the day of brotherly sharing", and collection boxes for this end are to be found in all Catholic and Protestant churches.

In the numerous associations formed to promote Judaeo-Christian cooperation, Catholics, Protestants and Jews work together for the promotion of better relationships between the Church and Judaism.

Finally, mention should be made of the enthusiasm in the theological faculties for joint effort at the scholarly level. Recently two series of books have been launched from the Catholic side with the object of furthering ecumenical research (*Ökumenischen Forschungen* edited by Hans Küng and Joseph Ratzinger, and *Beiträge zur ökumenischen Theologie,* edited by Heinrich Fries). The Johann Adam Möhler Institute in Paderborn is also doing valuable work in this field. The best known and most useful Catholic ecumenical journals are *Una Sancta* and *Catholica;* on the Protestant side, the most valuable is *Ökumenische Rundschau.* In this connection, mention should also be made of *Herder-Korrespondenz* and *Evangelischen Kommentare.*

Twice yearly, Munich University's Institute of Ecumenical Theology and Erlangen University's Faculty of Protestant Theology organize a theological conference. At these, attempts are made to determine what consequences will follow, with regard to joint theological research, from the well-known fact that the differences between the two Churches are basically ecclesiological. This joint theological work is primarily concerned with contemporary questions and the need to supply Christian answers to them.

ECUMENICAL EXPERIMENTS IN EAST GERMANY
Werner Becker, Leipzig, East Germany

In East Germany, the spawning ground of the Reformation, Protestants and Roman Catholics live cheek by jowl. Though in earlier times the Catholic minority (often less than 3%) attempted to establish itself as an exclusive diaspora community, the dominant tendency nowadays is for the two confessions to recognize their common diaspora situation as Christian vis-à-vis the world at large.

From 1945 onward, many thousands of Catholics were driven into East Germany from areas further east, and as a consequence the pastorate had to be structured afresh. From the start this was done in an ecumenical spirit. In town and country the newly arrived Catholic communities found themselves welcomed in Protestant churches, and through this situation contacts were made that are still proving their value now. The sharing of amenities by both clergy and people has led to a situation of friendship and trust in which the cares and joys of one community are shared by the other.

This, of course, has led to a number of events, both past and present, that together have done much to further Christian attitudes in everyday life. When in 1968 the diocese of Magdeburg —which, along with its suffragan dioceses of Merseburg, Zeitz-Naumburg and Meissen, was dissolved at the time of the Reformation—celebrated its millennium J. Gülden wrote: "We would like to celebrate this occasion in common with our fellow Christians of other confessions, insofar as this is possible in faith, hope and love." [1] The result was the celebration in Dresden on May 24 and September 1 of two happily complementary services that concluded with blessings dispensed jointly by the Roman Catholic and Protestant bishops present. In Dresden's

[1] Cf. J. Gülden, "Katholisches Hausbuch," in *Jahr des Herrn* [17] (Leipzig, 1968), Foreword.

Kreuzkirche, Protestant representatives proclaimed Pope Paul VI's act of contrition, and the duty of combining in the interests of the non-Christian world was endorsed as the new dimension of Christian hope based upon a common future. The Lutheran bishop Noth preached during the eucharist in the Catholic Hofkirche. Protestants in all large cities in the diocese of Meissen offered their church halls as places where members of both confessions could celebrate the Dresden millennium.

Also unprecedented was the way in which the 450th anniversary of the Reformation was celebrated in 1967. The high point of the major festivities in Wittenberg was an ecumenical conference during which a telegram of greeting from the late Cardinal Bea was read to the World Lutheran Federation. Study days in which Catholics took part, as well as ecumenical services for the young and for students, were arranged, and at the closing ceremony in Wittenberg the recent flowering of Catholic sympathy for Luther's objectives was described as the most exciting development of the festivities as a whole.

These ecumenical initiatives, first-fruits of a deepening awareness of a shared history, are not, strictly speaking, "ecumenical experiments": the Churches have more or less been driven to it by close proximity and common sense. For twenty years now hundreds of Catholic communities have had no churches of their own, and from what at first may have seemed to be an emergency solution to this problem—namely, the sharing of physical amenities provided by friendly Protestant communities—has grown the view that the next obvious step is the recognition of common pastoral responsibilities. Whereas for several years priests and lecturers in theology have come together for study days, the latest development has been for pastoral activities—for instance, in the new estates that circle the big cities, to be jointly undertaken; retreat days for the clergy are also being held in common. When the closing of the jointly used Universitätskirche in Leipzig left the provost and his congregation homeless, provost and people were ceremoniously inducted in the Protestant Nikolaikirche during an ecumenical service.

In 1954 Father Franz Stahlschmidt started a group whose members promised daily prayers for Christian unity, in the spirit of Christian Unity Week. This society has now been enlarged to form an ecumenical union, all of whose members offer such prayers, and a Protestant priest has joined Father Stahlschmidt in the running of the society. Guides for ecumenical prayer meetings have been produced by student communities,[2] whose strong tradition in this respect dates from 1947.

On January 18, 1969, Cardinal Bengsch presided jointly with Bishop Schönherr, representative of the Protestant bishops, at a liturgical service in St. Hedwigskathedrale, Berlin. The texts for the prayers for occasions such as these will in the future be produced by a Catholic and a Protestant publisher jointly.

The formation in 1958 on the initiative of Father K. Herbst, with the assistance of Protestant clergy, of a writing group, has brought the two communities yet closer together. The group now numbers over a thousand, most of them clergy, and not only sends out circulars and news sheets but also circulates each month a passage from Scripture for meditation purposes, and organizes an annual conference. The exchange of catechisms and ecumenically significant literature has also proved its worth.

Activities of this type were given fresh impetus by Vatican Council II. The many conferences organized across the length and breadth of the country by bishops and other participants at the Council aroused considerable interest among the Protestants, particularly at meetings of their clergy.

In January of this year the Protestant sodality of St. Michael invited representatives of all Christian societies and religious orders active in East Germany to take part in a study week during which they would examine their common roots.

Another consequence of the new spirit aroused by Vatican Council II is that the Evangelische Bund (The Evangelical Federation) has recently begun to invite Catholics to take part in its

[2] Cf. W. Trilling and W. Muschick, "Ökumenischer Gottesdienst in Leipzig," in *Katholische Studentenseelsorge: Geschichte und Gestalt,* ed. P. Benkart and W. Ruf (Paderborn, 1965), pp. 194-97.

study weeks. The research center this organization established in Potsdam enjoys the friendliest of relations with the Ecumenical Project Center founded by the Bishop of Meissen in Leipzig. It is also significant that the only review of the results of Vatican Council II to have appeared in East Germany comes from U. Kühn, a Protestant writer (Berlin, 1967).

The Protestant Bible Society of Berlin used the occasion of its 150th anniversary to include the Catholic translation of the New Testament by Franz Tillmann in its *Tetrapla*. At its conference in Berlin on March 19, 1968, a Catholic was invited to read a paper for the first time.

Since Vatican Council II it has been the case that the more lively a community is in the organization of its work through its various working groups, the more open it has shown itself to ecumenical objectives. This is also true of youth work. There are student communities that, in furtherance of an already existing tradition, have prepared programs covering a whole semester and have often exchanged their lecturers.

Since the Council, many new ecumenically orientated groups, often also ecumenical in composition, have been established. Thus, for instance, groups of Catholic and Protestant students in Leipzig have initiated a "Unity Action Group".

The action group founded in 1958 by L. Kreyssig (*Aktion Sühnezeichen*) has been of particular value to young people of both confessions since Vatican Council II. Since 1960 another action group (formed to fight world hunger) has operated in association with Kreyssig's group under the direction of a Catholic layman.

There are many other things I could mention: joint action against world hunger; regular consultation among the Churches at episcopal level (in which controversial issues such as the conditional baptism of converts have been discussed); the ecumenical work done by Catholic officials in the pastoral field; teachers in senior schools forming themselves into work groups for in-service training in ecumenical theology; exchange of contacts among the theological teaching centers, leading on occasion to the exchange of faculty members; the increasingly ecumenical orientation of theological formation; and so on.

It is now recognized with ever-increasing clarity that openness to the world is vital to the future of ecumenical endeavor. And here it is precisely the sort of experience thrust upon us by virtue of our particular situation that enables us to understand better than would be possible in many other places that ecclesiastical insularity in any one confession necessarily implies a loss of relevance to the world at large. "The situation in East Germany is ideally suited to the establishment of decent relationships among the confessions and facilitates the process of pressing on to the heart of the matter" [3]—which, of itself, means both opportunity and obligation.

———————————————

## ECUMENICAL EXPERIMENTS IN FRANCE
René Beaupère, O.P., Lyon, France

Ecumenism "in the concrete" is developing in France along three principal lines.

1. *Biblical Work in Common.* An ecumenical edition of the Bible has been in preparation for five years, and the hope is that it will be finished in 1975. It is of interest because it is radical; the translators' first idea was to start off from an already existing version and to be content with modifying that. They ended by choosing to do something really new. Their work in common makes it clear that disagreements arise most often not from divergencies of doctrine but from the differing points of view of various schools of exegesis.

This initiative was accompanied by the adoption, in 1966, of a common text of the *Our Father.* Unfortunately, one cannot yet say the same for the *Credo* and the *Apostles' Creed.* In the same

[3] Cf. U. Kühn, "Brüderliches Aufbruck," in *Jahr des Herrn, op. cit.,* pp. 243ff.

way we are looking forward to a movement of ecumenical catechesis for children and young people, especially but not exclusively among married couples of mixed religion. But nothing
really significant has yet been achieved in this field.

The new translation of the Scriptures that is being prepared
has, on the other hand, given a new impetus to interdenominational groups working on the Bible. Some of them have also been
helped and stimulated by correspondence courses from *Formation Oecumenique Interconfessionnelle* (F.O.I.), edited since
1966 by a team of Protestants, Catholics and Orthodox for all
French-speaking Christians.[1] One of these numerous courses is
concerned precisely with the "Ecumenical Preaching of the
Bible".

Ecumenical pilgrimages to the Holy Land have likewise given
rise to biblical groups of this kind. In any case, these pilgrimages,
whether to Palestine for background to rereading the Old and
New Testaments, or to Asia Minor or further to relive the history
of the Church, have a value in themselves—that of bringing
separated Christians to *live together* for a few weeks.[2]

2. *The Apostolate of Mixed Marriages.* It was in 1962 that the
first groupings of such couples were formed in France, and over
the last six years they have greatly increased; they are to be found
nowadays in very many large cities. Furthermore, the *Centre de
Villémetrie,* the abbeys of Ligugé and Bec, and the Community
of Taizé provide retreats for such couples or weekends for
reflection.

In towns and districts where no such groups have yet been set
up, there is a move to develop a common apostolate, with pastors
and priests in collaboration, especially in the preparation of
engaged couples for marriage.

This indispensible cooperation arose out of the initiative of a
few married couples, a few pastors and a few priests. But it is now
supported and promoted by all the ecclesiastical authorities,

---

[1] *Formation oecuménique interconfessionnelle* (F.O.I.)

[2] René Beaupère (ed.), *Protestants et catholiques en marche. Les pè-
lerinages oecuméniques au Pays de la Bible* (Paris, 1967); Jean Gabries,
*Le Caravansérail* (ed. Robert Morel, 1968).

which together published a brochure in June 1968.[3] This constitutes one of the most positive official ecclesiastical documents published until now anywhere in the world on the question of mixed marriages, and was made possible only by the experimentation that went before it; one can reasonably expect that it will in its own turn contribute to the wider diffusion of the benefits arising from this common apostolate.

Struck by the ignorance frequently shown by couples and by the clergy itself concerning the attitudes of the Churches in this field, and wanting to share their experiences with others, especially with fiancés or married couples living in isolation, some couples of mixed religion from Lyon and Switzerland took a new initiative in the autumn of 1968 with the active cooperation of their spiritual advisers and founded a quarterly bulletin devoted entirely to their problems.[4]

In this way, couples of mixed religion, with full commitment to the life of their respective Churches (their number is growing in relation to that of couples living on the periphery of ecclesiastical communities) are nowadays playing a dynamic role in ecumenism.

3. *Presence to the World.* Many ecumenical experiments of the most varied kinds are also under way in France in the fields of Christian witness, charities, and social, economic and political action. There are many examples, as much on the local as on the regional level. Such action is being inserted within the very structures of movements and organizations, in the form of a tendency to "interdenominationalize". For example *Témoinage Chretién,* a Catholic weekly whose editorial board includes one Dominican and one pastor, now has an opposite number in the Protestant movement *Christianisme Sociale,* which, in the spring of 1968, elected to its board a different Dominican.

Even more significant is the activity of CIMADE, an organization for mutual aid and development, which, starting as Prot-

[3] *Pastorale commune des foyers mixtes. Recommendations de le l'Eglise catholique et des Eglises reformees et lutheriennes de France* (Paris-Lyon, 1968).
[4] *Foyers mixtes,* a quarterly bulletin.

estant (and Orthodox) at its inception thirty years ago, has gradually become interdenominational; in the teams it has at work both in France and abroad, many Catholics are laboring side by side with Protestants and Orthodox. The movement has drawn the logical conclusion from this evolution by altering its constitution and inviting several Catholic personalities to sit on its board.

Intercommunion is a question to which theologians and ecclesiastical authorities alike gave insufficient attention before their eyes were abruptly opened by the communal celebration that occurred at Paris in June 1968 and forced them to take a serious look at it; there are good grounds for saying that intercommunion is now and will be increasingly a stumbling block.

These little teams, to which certain others should be added, in particular those formed among young people by the Community of Taizé, are, without any doubt at all, the humble workshops in which is being worked out the design for what the Churches—the renewed Church—will look like tomorrow.

---

ECUMENICAL EXPERIMENTS IN THE
NETHERLANDS AND BELGIUM
Wim Boelens, S.J., Stadskanaal, Netherlands

In order to understand the ecumenical experiments that are being tried out locally in Holland and Belgium, one should keep in mind that the ecclesiastical authorities there are at present very favorably disposed toward an ecumenical *rapprochement* and support it *via* official organizations. The most important body for mutual consultation at the highest ecclesiastical level in order to promote cooperation in study and pastoral work in Holland is the national Council of Churches, which has nine Churches and Christian communities as members and which was set up on June 21, 1968. This Council of Churches replaces the Ecumenical Council of Churches, in which membership was restricted to only those Churches which already belonged to the World Council of Churches. This no longer fitted the Dutch situation where the Roman Catholic and the Reformed Churches already worked closely together.

Such cooperation required a national structure which anticipated the development of the situation at world level. The World Council showed every understanding for this kind of pluriformity. Within the context of this top-level consultation, the Roman Catholic Church, the Dutch Reformed Church, other Reformed Churches and the Evangelical Lutheran Church agreed to recognize each other's baptism in 1967/8. This recognition implies the recognition of a basic Christian profession of faith which is now being worked out and which will lead before long to pastoral agreements concerning such issues as mixed marriages.

To correspond to this national Council of Churches, there is an increasing number of local Councils of Churches in various towns. As at national level, so here at local level the member Churches no longer undertake "to do separately what can be done together without insuperable objections in principle". Thus, in several large cities like Amsterdam, Rotterdam and Groningen, plans are currently being studied for setting up communal churches and communal centers for social service. A common approach has been made to the civic authorities in order to obtain effective subsidies, among other things. Often, however, there are still severe tensions. An important condition for the success of a local Council of Churches, in which each ecclesial community is represented by two members and where the lay element prevails, is the work of the interdenominational conventions of Church officers. These conventions exist in many places with a mixed Christian population, particularly in the predominantly Protestant North. Here dogmatic or pastoral subjects are discussed. The Council of Churches is a real step forward, because broader sections of the community are involved and the friendly, yet inconclusive element of the simple "conversation" is overcome.

The problem has been even more effectively tackled at the grass-roots level through the work of inter-Church discussion groups which have been spreading rapidly during the last two years, particularly in the North. A special commission, consisting of official representatives of members of the Council of Churches, has stimulated the formation of such groups at the grass-roots level in the diocese of Groningen. Some ten or twelve members of various Churches meet about four times during the winter season and discuss subjects concerning the practical life of the Christian in the modern world. The matter for these discussions is also organized by an interdenominational commission and handed out in the form of pamphlets. These groups were started by Roman Catholics in order to let the community make its contribution in an independent and critical way within the framework of the Pastoral Council. Just as the study commissions of the Pastoral Council, which compose the discussion reports for the plenary assembly three times a year, have invited members of other Churches to collaborate, so the bishop of Groningen wanted to invite Protestant Christians to this communal consultation. This process has developed in such a way that the work of the discussion groups is now being looked after and led by several Churches on equal footing.

When one begins to recognize the deeper implications of the other Churches' character as belonging to the "Church of Christ" and the relative character of one's own ecclesiality, one abandons the claim to "convert non-Catholic Christians. The "Open Doors" have become specialized institutes for ecumenical living together and discussion, whatever the atmosphere that surrounds those who want to become Catholic.

Beyond this, Christians are experiencing a communal responsibility for those who live on the fringe of or outside the Church as well as for non-Christians. This has led to an interdenominational review for evangelization which appears at Christmas and Easter. Interdenominational carol services at Christmas time have been going on for many years in many towns, and many fringe members take part in them. This phenomenon appears also in Belgium which has only about 50,000 Protestants and where most of the work is done through study commissions. Mutual understanding and the growth toward each other at the spiritual level are still more effectively fostered by the already traditional interdenominational vesper services which take place in several towns. Although the number of participants is usually small, there is a growing group of people who have an understanding for modern liturgy, and this liturgy is composed by progressive elements of the various Churches.

It is becoming increasingly common for a Protestant community to invite a Catholic priest to preach at the Sunday service. This happens less often the other way around, since it would imply a higher degree of *communicatio in sacris*—namely, cooperation within the context of a eucharistic celebration. Smaller groups (which occasionally number as many as 100 members) sometimes want to have a service which is not merely a service of the Word and points to intercommunion. For instance, at the end of a year's work in a discussion group, the members meet for an agape celebration where the strictly religious element is given fuller expression through the reading of Scripture, talks, the reading of secular news items, and singing together. The Sjaloom group has had an inspiring influence here. Occasionally this celebration comes formally and intentionally close to a sacramental eucharistic celebration in the strict sense. In any case, one can say that these agape celebrations provide a powerful stimulus toward serious thought about—and creating a definite desire for—such conditions as are required for intercommunion.

While one may rightly think that, in matters of doctrine, liturgy and the reform of Church order, the Roman authorities have been an obstacle rather than an inspiration for modern adaptation, it should be recognized that their decisions about mixed marriage offer great opportunities if interpreted constructively. This is evident from the pastoral letter of the Dutch hierarchy to their clergy on March 7, 1968, which stated that the priest will not mention the demand for a Catholic education of the children, including baptism and the Catholic school, in his pastoral talk to the partners. After consideration of all the circumstances, he will leave the decision to the parents. In every case where he can answer for the situation, he will be certain to receive the dispensation from the bishops. If the partners desire a Catholic blessing of the marriage, this celebration will usually only end with the eucharistic celebration if the Protestant partner can in his own conscience take communion. In this letter the bishops created this possibility by appealing to n. 8 of the *Decree on Ecumenism* as well as to n. 55 of *Directorium Oecumenicum* of May 14, 1967, provided that "he is baptized, can accept the Catholic belief in the Eucharist and is admitted to communion in his own Church".

The ecumenical situation is at present favorable enough to make the Protestant minister accept a liturgical function at the Catholic wedding. In that case he will at least give the sermon and hand over the rings with the appropriate prayer, while the priest functions as the main celebrant and demands the partners' consent. When, however, there is an objection to a wedding before a priest and two witnesses, the bishops can take care of the dispensation required, as they concluded from their dealings with the Roman authorities.

Finally, mention must be made of top-level consultation about action for world peace, embodied in the national "Inter-Church Council for Peace". Among other things, this Council organizes an annual week for peace. During this week there are local interdenominational services for peace, occasionally interdenominational peace pilgrimages for young people, and a discussion about the problems of peace that is concluded with a "forum" discussion.

Unfortunately, national consultation about a common translation of the Bible has not yet led to concrete results, apart from the Frisian province where there is a Frisian edition. There is cooperation in Bible promulgation, and there are also "Bible

Kiosks", organized for local festivities, if the opportunity presents itself.

Contact in missionary and development work is making slow progress, in common education as well as in matters of publicity and collections. Occasionally there are collections for a missionary of another Church.

In the matter of interdenominational catechetics, there is now a common check on historically wrong interpretations in each other's history books, and there are also interdenominational discussions for youth groups, while different ministers are allowed to function occasionally in the various catechetical classes held in denominational schools.

## ECUMENICAL EXPERIMENTS IN ITALY
Maria Vingiani, Rome, Italy

The special religious position of Italy explains why most people are either indifferent to or suspicious of the ecumenical movement. Furthermore, the existence of few Orthodox communities, the character and the behavior of the Italian Evangelicals (an attitude usually critical of the Catholic Church and of Italian religious life in general, psychological obstacles and historical experiences which weigh heavily on the Waldensians, intrusive proselytism by movements and sects, clumsy publicity and slanted appraisals of reports of disagreements among Catholics), and, on the Catholic side, a deep-seated triumphalistic mentality, the use of dialectics without dialogue, intolerance and, above all, mutual ignorance— all these factors have made and continue to make the path of ecumenism a difficult one.

In spite of this, there has been for some time, even in Italy, an improvement in the approach toward the subject, thanks largely to the work of pioneers and more or less organized groups on the evangelical as well as on the Catholic side. We refer to the activities and writings of the Waldensians Janni and Miegge, to the Protestant experience of the ecumenical village of Agape and the national movements of the U.C.D.G., to the work of Catholic associations, reviews, religious groups (*Unitas,* Foyer Unitas, Lega di preghiera, *Oriente cristiano, Russia cristiana,* and others) as well as a few advanced diocesan secretariats (Pinerolo), cultural and spiritual reviews and centers (Il Gallo in Genoa, the Movimento dei Focolari, and others). Naturally, the ecumenical directions of the Council have caused the above groups and activities to develop and to bring their work up to date. They have stimulated theological and biblical studies (mixed meetings of Catholic and Protestant clergy in Milan and Turbin) as well as liturgical, catechetical and pastoral renewal. They have also led to the foundation of study and research centers (John XXIII Study Circle at Sotto il Monte, the Koinonia Centre in Rome, the Jewish-Christian Friendship Circle in Florence) and ecumenical centers of prayer and encounter. The "Centro Uno" and "Ut unum sint" collaborate in the publication of a new ecumenical review, and a number of publishing houses such as Morcelliana, Il Mulino, Queriniana, Gribaudi, Cittadella, etc, now specialize in the production of books on ecumenical subjects. Recently there has been a first unofficial attempt to translate the Bible with the assistance of experts of every denomination, and thanks to the efforts of the C.E.I. (the Italian Episcopal Conference), the ecumenical edition of the Bible is now being prepared. To this may be added the appointment at a slow pace of the diocesan ecumenical commissions, and the study weeks on the problem which this year have been organized for the clergy at the instigation of Bishop G. Marafini, who is responsible to the Italian Episcopal Conference for ecumenism in Italy.

The seminaries and faculties of theology have done very little, and there is a noticeable attempt to adopt a negative attitude and apply the brakes. In actual fact, many Catholics are ignorant of ecumenism. Others do not understand it or refuse to accept it. Its dangers are exaggerated and the harm caused by rejecting it is ignored. In too many cases it is reduced to an irenic and conservative formula, thus preventing it from expanding and manifesting itself for what it is: the "hour" of God, the place and the time when we are, all of us, individuals and Churches alike, called upon to convert and reform ourselves.

Things are no better on the Protestant side. In most cases the ecumenical experience has been rejected before it has been thoroughly tested because of a persistence in misjudging the true state of affairs inside the Catholic Church and the genuineness of her ecumenical commitment. Thus the necessary grass-roots experience of ecumenism has been missing—namely, that open and loyal relationship which fosters knowledge and dialogue with the object of furthering the common Christian service, which is what is demanded by the second stage of ecumenism.

In both cases, however, there are extenuating circumstances. In Italy, as everywhere else, religious anxiety is widespread. Within all Churches there is the problem of the dissent of the young who press for the speed-up of the building of the world of tomorrow. Ecumenism, it is feared, will be used to call into question loyalty to one's own Church and to criticize its structures, its worship and its preaching. Furthermore, there is a very serious obstacle to dialogue and collaboration. Immediately World War II, owing to an error of an opposite nature, Catholics and Protestants fell victims to a political situation which, because it forced a choice between clericalism and anti-clericalism, secularism and sectarianism, created a further breach between Christians when called upon to fulfill their commitments as citizens and patriots. For this reason, the ecumenical situation is critical. Far from being static, it is the subject, in the more responsible Catholic and non-Catholic circles, of ever growing concern, but it is critical, perhaps because it is in the process of growth and is endeavoring to find its way. Catholics and Christians of every denomination are urgently aware of the need to give a common evangelical reply and witness to the problems of peace, justice, liberty, revolution, education, the renewal of structures, hunger, the third world, and so on, but on account of their different mentality, they find that they argue and disagree in their judgments—hence the need to insist on the fundamental problem of the "reform of mentality", so that a path toward ecumenism can be cleared.

For this reason a special answer has come spontaneously from the laity who, from the very beginning, have understood the call for Christian unity not as an aim in itself, but as an historic occasion for rediscovering together and bearing witness to the evangelical values of liberty, truth, justice and peace, from which alone the world can expect progress and salvation. This is the fundamental reason for the service of the Segretariato Attivita Ecumeniche (S.A.E.) (Secretariat for Ecumenical Activities) which I will mention briefly. In 1946, in the divided and anxious atmosphere of the first electoral meetings (during which they had clashed in opposite political parties) a group of Catholic laymen, together with Evangelicals and Jews, organized privately a series of mixed meetings for the purpose of getting to know each other, exchange ideas and draw up lines of conduct for the social and religious integration of the local community. From the beginning, the group had a triple objective clearly in mind: (1) to secure the reconciliation between Christians, at least as far as relations are concerned, basing it on the common message of the Bible and of Israel; (2) make reparation for the grave crimes of anti-Semitism, which are not without Christian roots; (3) to give life to brotherly and friendly relations between Christians and Jews and search together for common solutions to the problems of our times.

True to these aims, these meetings which were promoted thanks to Catholic initiative and were privately authorized by hierarchical authority (Cardinal Patriarchs Piazza, Roncalli, Urbani) widened their sphere of operations as soon as Pope John announced that the Council had a clear ecumenical aim, and they organized themselves officially in Rome as a national movement of laymen committed to the ecumenical education of the laity. For this purpose, the S.A.E. has promoted certain kinds of experiments. For those who are interested in the problems of dialogue, it organizes open debates and study groups on such subjects as religious liberty, mixed marriages, relations between Christians and Jews, proselytism and mission, and the theology of earthly reality. It establishes centers for ecumenical operations in the various dioceses of its members. It organizes annually a "National Session for the Ecumenical Training of the Laity" in which the doctrine in relation to the work of the group is expressed in terms of spiritual life in the "lectio divina". The attendance of the laity at the session, which lasts a week, is ever increasing (250 at the last meeting) and consists largely of students, graduates and professional men, which is the sphere to which S.A.E. has appealed from the beginning, because it is the one most concerned in working out with critical method the new cultural and spiritual directions.

The participation at these conferences of Jews, and Christians of other denominations, as experts and guests affords an insight into different outlooks on life not easily understood in Italy, and enriches the meeting with common prayer and the joyful experience of brotherly communion based on the unity which already exists and which yearns to be complete. The reports of the sessions are published regularly, so as to offer to a wider public doctrinal contributions of the meetings under such titles as "Ecumenism: The Vocation of the Church", "The Church", "The Church, Mystery and Sign of Unity", "Ecumenism and the History of Salvation", "Ecumenism and Dialogue," "Religious Liberty and Ecumenism". The subject for the next session is "Ecumenism and the Evangelization of Peace". In order to promote spiritual ecumenism, it also organizes prayer meetings, days of recollection and ecumenical pilgrimages through the intermediary of the diocesan circles, and with those who are concerned with the same problem. The work of the S.A.E. is conducted under the supervision of a permanent committee of ecclesiastical and lay experts who ensure that it operates in complete loyalty with the directions of the Church, but nevertheless it exercises its own autonomous responsibility regarding its choice of activities and service. Far from causing confusion and perplexity, the movement has witnessed in its adherents a growth of their commitment to the spiritual life and to the study of religious sciences and theology, because it is rooted in the conviction that ecumenism is gift and grace and therefore vocation.

---

ECUMENICAL EXPERIMENTS IN GREECE
Dimitri Salachas, Athens, Greece

Over the last few years, it can be said that in Greece, in spite of still existing reservations, relationships between Catholic and Orthodox [1] individuals have been characterized by genuine cordiality and a spirit of mutual respect. It must nonetheless be admitted that the official relationships of the two Churches have remained within the framework of everyday or formal contacts without any concrete ecumenical program, above all at the local level. As for any form of collaboration on the level of biblical studies, catechesis, common prayer and action for unity and a prudent making ready for eventual intercommunion, we must answer that there is none. Indeed there is a considerable distance to go in Greece before such a stage of ecumenism is reached. The reservations are mostly on the part of the Orthodox; for her part the Catholic Church would not lightly venture on any such initiatives because the atmosphere really does not favor it. But what are the motives underlying these reservations?

One must first of all realize that Greece is a free and Christian country in which Orthodoxy is "the dominant Church", whose thought and life are safeguarded and promoted within the framework of the tradition of Christian Hellenism. In our times Greece continues to be the effective center of contemporary Graeco-

---

[1] Cf. the article by Basil Exarchos in this volume of *Concilium*.

Christian civilization and thus considers herself to be the depository of the pure and authentic Byzantine tradition, the guardian of the Orthodox faith and of the continuity of Greek Orthodox theological thought. It is in virtue of this privileged position that the Church of Greece has exercised such an influence, and still does so, on the Orthodox Patriarchachates and Churches of the Middle East. She is conscious of being the nurse and protectress of the Orthodox faith, which it is her duty to preserve from every danger, both internal and external. If the Church of Greece has shown a certain reaction against and reserve toward the ecumenical movement and, above all, Catholicism, that is due precisely to this consciousness and to the task she has assumed of watching over and protecting the Orthodox faith. That is why she has also allowed herself from time to time to intervene and criticize the initiatives even of the ecumenical patriarchate, going so far as to reckon them "full of risk and peril, scandalizing the consciences of our Orthodox faithful and creating a grave hazard to our Orthodox faith and our Church".[2]

But why is there such a mistrust of Catholicism? Some time ago the late Mgr. Chrysostomos, archbishop of Athens and primate of Greece, gave this answer: "The fact is well known, and history bears witness to it, that the Roman Catholic Church has never abandoned her aim or renounced her intentions of bringing into subjection and submitting to papal authority our Orthodox Church. The decisions of Vatican Council II make perfectly plain the extent to which Catholicism is attached to this aim and to its pretensions. . . . Given this grave danger to our Orthodox Church, our holy synod has the duty and urgent responsibility to its Orthodox flock to protect it against all pernicious propaganda."[3] Mgr. Hieronymos, the present primate of Greece, gives for his part the following answer to the question: "This finds its explanation in history, one which still strongly influences the attitude of the Orthodox Greek people; this fact cannot be ignored. The Roman Church will have to behave toward the Church of Greece

[2] Encyclical Letter of the holy synod of the Church of Greece, n. 885, March 11, 1968.
[3] *Ibid.*

with brotherly friendship for a long time yet if the entire people are to believe that her attitude is genuinely brotherly and friendly." [4]

These motives, however, do not seem to explain everything, and indeed Mgr. Hieronymos, in his recent book on *The Reorganization of the Church of Greece,* has this to say concerning the attitude of people and clergy in Greece toward other Churches: "Concerning the heteredox, our knowledge is simply made up of generalities; everything else is unknown to us. We know them only from the pages of the polemical literature that deals with them. We know them as adversaries, and even that one-sidedly. The vast majority of the people have absolutely no knowledge of the heteredox Churches, or rather only that knowledge with which polemics against them have provided. As a result, it is manifest that the attitudes of the Orthodox faithful toward the heteredox are somewhat hostile." [5] The primate of Greece goes on to invite the Orthodox clergy and people to cultivate fraternal charity toward and mutual respect for their brethren of the Christian Churches and denominations. "It is in this way that friendship can be promoted while we keep intact our perseverance in the faith and in Orthodox doctrine." [6] It must however be said that nothing much has been done to enable the Greek Orthodox people to respond to this appeal from their archbishop.

In such a context it is very difficult to raise the question of shared acts of worship or of any form of prudent intercommunion between the two Churches. It is true that some efforts have been made in this direction by Catholic and Orthodox individuals—prayer in common, shared acts of worship—but these initiatives provoked the intervention of the holy synod of the Church of Greece. On April 16, 1967 every bishop received an encyclical letter from the holy synod on this question: "The holy synod observes, not without a certain anxiety, that in recent times certain venerable prelates have been countenancing official ecclesiastical

[4] The "Typos" Agency, n. 12, November 1967.
[5] Mgr. Hieronymos, *Plan for the Reorganization of the Church of Greece* (Athens, 1967), p. 62.
[6] *Ibid.,* p. 112.

contacts, common acts of worship and other expressions of good will with representatives and clergy of the heterodox Churches. These contacts, which go far beyond formal and established relations, are giving rise to many sorts of comment and are an occasion of scandal for the faithful of our Orthodox Church. Among some they arouse doubts and weaken the firmness of their faith and their Orthodox beliefs. For this reason the holy synod, in loyal continuity with past ages of the history of our Orthodox Church and ever on the watch to protect her faith and tradition, anxious to prevent for even one of her faithful any occasion whereby their Orthodox faith might be shaken, has come to the decision to draw the attention of bishops to this question of relationships with representatives and clerics of the heterodox Churches. The bishops are advised to cease any contacts that go beyond those imposed by social and customary obligations, and to put an end to any sort of shared worship and official ecclesiastical relations." [7] An encyclical was also issued in the same sense by the present holy synod in July 1967.[8] Furthermore it is not normal for the Orthodox Church to admit that there is even any possibility of "communicatio in sacris" between Orthodox and Catholic, in that "the holy eucharist is an offering and an act of worship celebrated by the Christian community in union with the priest and giving thanks to God through the offering made in unity and in communion of faith; it therefore presupposes the unity of Christians in faith and in truth. . . . The sharing of the faithful in one chalice constitutes the perfect expression of unity in faith. That is why the early Church invariably deprived of this sharing in 'the common cup' all those who had gone astray in the faith." [9]

As for any collaboration in the production of a common Bible, reservations still exist and are due to mistrust of "those ecumenical translations of dubious fidelity to the inspired text". Any ecumen

[7] Encyclical Letter of the holy synod of the Church of Greece, n. 1423, April 6, 1967.

[8] Encyclical Letter of the holy synod of the Church of Greece, n. 1446, July 13, 1967.

[9] Review *Anaplasis*, August, 1968.

ical collaboration on a common Bible could mean the alteration of the Orthodox faith.[10]

However, if the dialogue between Catholic and Orthodox in Greece is still in so rudimentary a stage, the reason is to be found largely in the resentment felt by the Orthodox with regard to the activities of the heterodox, above all of the Catholics who are accused of proselytism. "We make one condition," wrote Mgr. Hieronymos, "on which we are prepared to make no concessions, a necessary condition for any sort of close and fraternal relationship, and that is the absolute cessation of proselytism." [11] The Church of Greece remains, in effect, suspicious of the sincerity both of the World Council of Churches and its members, and of Catholicism. It was precisely this mistrust that prompted the holy synod and Mgr. Hieronymos to suggest the following clause for inclusion in the new Greek constitution: "Proselytism and any form of activity, direct or indirect, against the interests of the dominant Church are forbidden." [12] To this the holy synod annexed the following footnote: "Proselytism shall be deemed to include any sort of provision for, or service or attention to, any Orthodox Christian present within this country, that is made without the approval of the competent ecclesiastical authority, by any persons, groups, organizations, Churches or denominations that are not in communion, as laid down by the holy canons, with the Eastern Orthodox Church." [13] These suggestions were not incorporated by the government in the text of the constitution approved last September by the Greek people.

It is, however, worth asking whether this accusation is well founded. Does the Catholic Church proselytize among the Orthodox faithful in Greece? She has certainly never done anything to deceive or do violence to the conscience of our Orthodox brothers in order to bring them into the Catholic Church. But it is impossible to deny that in the past, by means of her charitable and pastoral work and in conformity with the general spirit of those

[10] Review O Sotir, October 16, 1968.
[11] Mgr. Hieronymos, op. cit., p. 112.
[12] Review Ekklisia, October 1968.
[13] Ibid.

times and the mentality that went with it, the Church worked for and promoted "the return of separated brethren" and their individual "conversion" to Catholicism. This provoked a violent reaction and a settled distrust among Orthodox circles that feared absorption by the Roman Church. Nor should it be forgotten that the foreign element in the Catholic clergy in Greece had something to do with the intensification of this mentality, one naturally out of touch with the new era in the relations of the Orthodox and Catholic Churches. Pope Paul VI, speaking of the meeting in Jerusalem, said that it had opened "a new age in the relations between the Holy see and the venerable ecumenical patriarchate". On the other hand, the *Decree on Ecumenism* has provided a basis on which new relations between the Catholic and Orthodox Churches both can and ought to be developed, and we have begun to see, from both Churches, actions that are, in the biblical sense of the term, "signs", inspired by the rediscovery that they are sister-Churches.

The Catholic Church continues to bear her Christian witness through her activities and ecumenical spirit. It is not within her power to renounce her own identity and life remaining passive and inert, to deny the ontological imperative of her own existence and reality. She cannot renounce the preaching of the Word, the spreading of the doctrine of Christ, or all the works of charity and of evangelism whereby she puts herself at the service of mankind. The accusation of proselytism cannot today be justly leveled against the Catholic Church, and it can no longer be used as a pretext for reserve and mistrust.

What is the outlook for ecumenism in Greece? It is hard to say. For the moment the Greek clergy and people, both Catholic and Orthodox, are moving slowly forward between enthusiasm and reserve, good will and mistrust, persistent prejudice and the desire for common action, the opening up of new horizons for the young and the traditionalism of the old. One thing is certain: at the moment Greece is going through a far-reaching transformation at every level of her social, political, economic and cultural life, and we have good reasons to think that this transformation will ultimately issue into an ecumenical activity and commitment. Ecumenical work and initiatives must arise from an ecumenical consciousness in both people and clergy. Such a consciousness is slowly and progressively taking shape in Greece.

---

ECUMENICAL EXPERIMENTS IN AFRICA AND ASIA
Steven Mackie, Geneva, Switzerland

The number and variety of ecumenical initiatives in the field of mission is growing rapidly. Since 1963, the World Council of Churches, through its Division of World Mission and Evangelism, has had a program of Joint Action for Mission, the aim of which has been to encourage Churches working in a specific geographical area to *survey* together the needs and opportunities confronting them, to *plan* together for the joint use of their common resources, and to initiate projects of joint *action*. Some of these projects are now in operation. In many of them the cooperating Churches include the Roman Catholic Church and other Churches which are not members of the World Council of Churches. In order to give some idea of the range of such projects, four such initiatives are herein described, three from Africa and one from Asia.

1. The field of *urban and industrial evangelism* is relatively new, at least as far as Asia and Africa are concerned, and many of the ventures in this field have been ecumenical from the start. One such example is in the new industrial town of Durgapur in West Bengal, India, where an Ecumenical Industrial Team Ministry was established in 1965 supported by the Anglican, Baptist and Methodist Churches and by the United Church of North India. An Ecumenical Social and Industrial Institute was set up at the same time with social and economic research, joint planning and laity training among its aims. It also sponsors a training course for pastors in urban and industrial work. Par-

ticipants of the eleven-week course in the spring of 1968 included Roman Catholic as well as Anglican priests together with members from the Methodist Church, the Church of South India and the United Church of North India.

2. A similar project in Tema, Ghana, related to the West African Industrial Mission of the All-Africa Conference of Churches, has a planning committee with representatives of the Salvation Army, of the Anglican, Methodist, Lutheran, Presbyterian, and Roman Catholic Churches, and of the African Methodist Episcopal Zion Church. The work of the Tema Industrial Mission includes the training of Bible study groups in a soap factory, community organization, service to seamen, civic education, vocational training and a training course for trade union officials. Some of these activities are carried on in collaboration with secular agencies, both public and private, including the university and other educational institutions.

3. A consultation on "The Evangelization of West Africa Today" was held at Yaoundé, Cameroon, in June 1965 following a survey of 21 nations in West and Equatorial Africa undertaken by the Division of World Mission and Evangelism together with the All-Africa Conference of Churches. The survey disclosed many unevangelized or largely unevangelized areas. One of these was in the Fon country in Eastern Dahomey. Under the name of *Action Apostolique Commune* a group of some 18 French-speaking Protestant Churches in Africa, Madagascar, Europe and Polynesia set up a committee with a Malagasy chairman and a Togolese secretary to send an international evangelistic team into Dahomey. The team includes an evangelist from the Methodist Church in Dahomey, a youth-worker from Tahiti, an elementary teacher from Madagascar, a Swiss nurse, a social worker from Togo and two pastors, one from Cameroon and one from France. Of the initial budget, 45% is being raised by Churches in Africa, Madagascar and the Pacific. The team has been at work in the area around Bohicon in the interior of Dahomey since early 1968.

4. A different kind of initiative is being taken in the *medical*

field, as, for instance, in Malawi, where a survey of Church-related hospitals (both Protestant and Catholic) was undertaken in 1965 at the request of the Malawi Christian Council. As a result of this survey, the Private Hospital Association of Malawi was established, with a view to joint planning and to a gradual sharing of resources. The Executive Committee is equally divided between Roman Catholics on the one hand and Protestants and Anglicans on the other. There is now a permanent staff of two —a Roman Catholic sister from Holland and a Protestant hospital administrator from the United States. The Association has two main objectives: (1) one central hospital, regardless of ownership, becomes the referral base for specialized clinical care, offering the possibility of consultation and advice to outlying institutions and using them as outreach facilities for public health and health education programs; (2) to improve the standards of training programs. Since the government raised the standard of nursing education to the State Registered Nurse level, no Church-related hospital possesses all the facilities and professional personnel to qualify. By joint action and the sharing of trained personnel, it is now hoped to establish such a school which will train nurses for all the hospitals. Member hospitals also engage in joint planning and development with a mutual review of all projects and plans. They purchase their supplies in bulk and make one collective representation to the government for grants. This kind of cooperation is likely to become more common with the founding of the Christian Medical Commission as a sponsored agency of the DWME but in close touch with Roman Catholic institutes.

---

## CONCLUSION

One of the questions put to our authors was: What part does the younger generation play in the ecumenical movement of your country? Do they perhaps show another view of ecumenism?

None of the authors replied to these questions. This is the more regrettable when one remembers that more than half of the world's population consists of young people under twenty-five. Some authors have pointed to the ecumenical movement among university students while Jeffery, Becker and Mejía mention some concrete results in ecumenism among the young in general. Probably ecumenism has already become so obvious to the young that they presuppose it. Perhaps, too, their interest turns rather to problems that are more actual for them, such as revolution, the third world and economic justice for all. Last year in Uppsala the youth delegation observed that youth is not so much the hope of the future as the future is the hope of youth, and that a society which builds for its future has no youth problem. But does the Church not build up the future precisely through the ecumenical movement? Does it not become more "inhabitable" and attractive after the ecumenical expansion?

The attentive reader of this volume will surely be convinced that, by breaking down the barriers, the ecumenical movement has not only obeyed the evangelical message about unity among Christians but has also opened up a broader vision for the future. The basic question which young people always ask themselves is whether there is still room for a future in an institutional Church. It would be a pity if the contribution of the young to an inspiring future would remain separate from what the ecumenical movement in the Churches has already achieved insofar as hope for the future is concerned. If ecumenism is a form of dialogue, then here, too, what is said of all dialogue must remain valid—namely, that it is the gathering of heirs around an undivided heritage.

# BIOGRAPHICAL NOTES

JEAN-JACQUES VON ALLMEN: Born in Lausanne in 1917, he was ordained in the Reformed Church in 1941. He studied in Switzerland at the universities of Lausanne, Basle and Neuchâtel, receiving his doctorate in theology in 1948. He is professor of theology at the faculty of theology at the University of Neuchâtel. His publications include *Prophétisme sacramentel* (Neuchâtel, 1964) and *Essai sur le repas du Seigneur* (Neuchâtel, 1966).

HERMAN FIOLET: Born in the Netherlands in 1920, he was ordained in 1946. He studied at the Catholic University of Nijmegen, receiving his doctorate in theology in 1953. He is secretary of studies of the Catholic Association for Ecumenism and editorial secretary of the review *Oecumene*. His published works include *Onyermoed perspectief op de Oecumene* (Hilversum, 1963) and *Dilemma doorbroken* (Hilversum, 1965).

WALTER ABBOTT, S.J.: Born in America in 1923, he was ordained in 1956. He studied at Boston College and Weston College in America, and at Oxford University, gaining his M.A. and licentiates in philosophy and theology. As a member of the Secretariat in Rome for the Promotion of Christian Unity, he is director of ecumenical collaboration on the Bible. He is editor of *The Documents of Vatican II* (London and New York, 1966) and one of the authors of the forthcoming work *A Bible Reader* (London, 1969).

JOS LESCRAUWAET, M.S.C.: Born in Amsterdam in 1923, he was ordained in 1948. He studied at the Catholic University of Nijmegen, receiving his doctorate in theology. He has been professor of dogma at the theological faculty of Tilburg in Holland since 1967. His published works include *De Bijbel over de christelijke eenheid* (1961) and *Compendium van het Oecumenisme* (Roermond-Maaseik, 1962).

MARTIN REARDON: Born in England in 1932, he was ordained in the Anglican Church in 1958. He studied in England at the University of Cambridge and at the Cuddesdon Theological College of Oxford, as well as at the Ecumenical Institute of Bossey in Geneva and the University of Louvain. He has been secretary of the Sheffield Council of Churches since 1962. In collaboration with Kenneth Greet, he published *Social Questions* (1964).

JOHN DILLENBERGER: Born in America in 1918, he was ordained in the United Church of Christ in 1943. He studied in America at Elmhurst

College, the Union Theological Seminary and Columbia University, receiving his doctorate in philosophy. He is dean of the Graduate Theological Union of Berkeley, California, president of the editorial board of *A Library of Protestant Thought,* and one of the editors of *Journal for Theology and the Church.* His published works include *Protestant Thought and Natural Science* (1960).

JOHN BENNETT: Born in America in 1902, he was ordained in the United Church of Christ in 1939. He studied in America at Williams College and the Union Theological Seminary, as well as at Oxford University, obtaining degrees in arts and theology. Holding honorary doctorates from numerous Anglo-Saxon universities, he is professor of social ethics at the Union Theological Seminary in New York and chairman of the editorial board of *Christianity and Crisis.* His published works include *Foreign Policy in Christian Perspective* (1966).

JAN WITTE, S.J.: Born in the Netherlands in 1907, he was ordained in 1940. He studied at the theological faculty of Maestricht in Holland and at Heidelberg University, receiving his doctorate in theology. He has been professor of Protestant and ecumenical theology at the Gregorian in Rome since 1955. He has published "Die Katholizitat der Kirche" in *Gregorianum* (1961), and contributes frequently to this journal.

MAURICE VILLAIN, S.M.: Born in France in 1900, he was ordained in 1927. He studied in Paris at the Sorbonne and at the School of Higher Studies, as well as at the Angelicum in Rome and the theological faculty of Lyons, receiving his doctorate in theology. Engaged in research on ecumenical theology, his publications include *Introduction a l'Oecuménisme* (Paris, 1961) and *Vatican II et le dialogue oecumenique* (Paris, 1966).

HEINZ ZAHRNT: Born in Germany in 1915, he was ordained in the Lutheran Evangelical Church in 1939. He studied theology and history, gaining his doctorate in theology. He is theological adviser to *Deutsche Allgemein Sonntagsblatt.* His published works include *Die Sache mit Gott, Protestantische Theologie im 20 Jahrhundert* (Munich, 1967) and *Gespräch über Gott. Ein Textbuch der Theologie* (1968).

LÉON-JOSEPH CARDINAL SUENENS: Born in Belgium in 1904, he was ordained in 1927, consecrated a bishop in 1945, and made a cardinal in 1962. He received his degree in Canon Law and doctorates in philosophy and theology. Since 1961 he has been archbishop of Malines-Brussels. He is the author of numerous books, the most recent being *Coresponsibility in the Church* (London & New York, 1969).

JOHANNES LILJE: Born in Germany in 1899, he was ordained in the Lutheran Evangelical Church in 1924. He studied theology and the history of art, receiving his doctorate in theology in 1932. He has also received honorary doctorates from a number of universities in Europe and America. He was consecrated a bishop of the Lutheran Evangelical

Church of Hannover in 1947, and has been president of the German Union of Lutheran Evangelical Bishops since 1950. His published works include *Atheismus, Humanismus, Christentum* (1962) and *Martin Luther* (Hamburg, 1964).

HUGH MONTEFIORE: Born in London in 1920, he was ordained in the Anglican Church in 1950. He studied at St. John's College, Oxford and at Westcott House, Cambridge. He holds degrees in the arts and theology, and is New Testament Reader at Cambridge University. In addition, he is vicar of the University Church of St. Mary the Great at Cambridge, and theological canon of Coventry Cathedral. His published works include *A Commentary on the Epistle to the Hebrews* (1964) and *Christ for Us Today* (1968).

HENDRIKUS BERKHOF: Born in the Netherlands in 1914, he is a member of the Dutch Reformed Church. He studied at the University of Leiden in Holland, receiving his doctorate in theology. He is professor of dogmatic and biblical theology at the University of Leiden, and editor of *Nederlands Theologisch Tijdschrift*. His published works include *De katholiciteit der Kerk* (1962) and *Gegronde Verwachting* (Nijkerk, 1967).

BASIL EXARCHOS: Born in Greece in 1903, he is a member of the Greek Orthodox Church. He studied at the universities of Athens, Hamburg and Leipzig, receiving his doctorate in theology. He is guest professor at the College of Catechetics at Esslingen in Germany. His publications include *Der Gegenstand der wissenschaftlichen Forschung im Rahmen der Theologischen Fakultät* (Thessalonica, 1951) and the forthcoming *Kirche und Atheismus in orthodoxer Sicht*.

DAVID BOWMAN, S.J.: Born in America in 1919, he was ordained in 1950. Holding a doctorate in theology, he has been co-director of the "Faith and Order Group" of the American National Council of Churches since 1966.

ROBERT JEFFERY: Born in England in 1935, he was ordained in the Anglican Church in 1959. He has been secretary of the Faith and Order Commission of the British Council of Churches since 1968.

JOHN COVENTRY, S.J.: Born in England in 1915, he was ordained in 1947. He received degrees in the arts and theology, and is dean of studies and lecturer in dogmatic theology at Heythrop College, Oxfordshire.

JORGE MEJÍA: Born in Buenos Aires in 1923, he was ordained in 1945. He earned his licentiate in Scripture and his doctorate in theology. He has been secretary of the Ecumenical Commission of the Latin American Episcopal Council (CELAM) since 1968.

JOHANNES BROSSEDER: Born in Germany in 1937, he is a Catholic. He is an assistant at the Institute of Ecumenical Theology of the University of Munich.

WERNER BECKER: Born in Germany in 1904, he was ordained in 1932. He holds doctorates in law and Canon Law and is president of the Diocesan Ecumenical Council of Leipzig.

RENÉ BEAUPÈRE, O.P.: Born in Lyons in 1925, he was ordained in 1951. He is a lecturer in theology, and director of the Ecumenical Centre of St. Irénée in Lyons, and also a director of *Lumière et Vie*.

WIM BOELENS, S.J.: Born in the Netherlands in 1925, he was ordained in 1958. He received his doctorate in theology, and is currently diocesan advisor on ecumenical contacts to the deaneries of Veendam and Mussel-kanaal in Holland.

MARIA VINGIANI: Born in Italy in 1924, she is a Catholic. She holds a doctorate in literature, and is professor of history and Italian literature at a college in Rome. She is founder-president of the Ecumenical Secretariat.

DIMITRI SALACHAS: Born in Athens in 1939, he was ordained in 1964. He studied in Rome at the Pontifical Propaganda University and at the Gregorian, and in Jerusalem at the Seminary of St. Anne. He holds degrees in philosophy and theology, and is director of the Catholic press agency "Typos" and secretary of the Greco-Catholic Exarchate.

STEVEN MACKIE: Born in Edinburgh in 1927, he was ordained in the Anglican Church in 1956. He holds degrees in the arts and theology, and is executive secretary of the Division of World Mission and Evangelism of the World Council of Churches.

## International Publishers of CONCILIUM

ENGLISH EDITION
Paulist Press
*Paramus, N.J., U.S.A.*

Burns & Oates Ltd.
25 Ashley Place
London, S.W.1

DUTCH EDITION
*Uitgeverij Paul Brand, N.V.*
*Hilversum, Netherlands*

FRENCH EDITION
Maison Mame
*Tours/Paris, France*

JAPANESE EDITION (PARTIAL)
Nansôsha
*Tokyo, Japan*

GERMAN EDITION
Verlagsanstalt Benziger & Co., A.G.
*Einsiedeln, Switzerland*

Matthias Grunewald-Verlag
*Mainz, W. Germany*

SPANISH EDITION
Ediciones Guadarrama
*Madrid, Spain*

PORTUGUESE EDITION
Livraria Morais Editora, Ltda.
*Lisbon, Portugal*

ITALIAN EDITION
Editrice Queriniana
*Brescia, Italy*

POLISH EDITION (PARTIAL)
Pallottinum
*Poznan-Warsaw, Poland*